Change Your Life with NLP

Prentice Hall LIFE

If life is what you make it, then making it better starts here.

What we learn today can change our lives tomorrow. It can change our goals or change our minds; open up new opportunities or simply inspire us to make a difference. That's why we have created a new breed of books that do more to help you make more of *your* life.

Whether you want more confidence or less stress, a new skill or a different perspective, we've designed *Prentice Hall Life* books to help you to make a change for the better. Together with our authors we share a commitment to bring you the brightest ideas and best ways to manage your life, work and wealth.

In these pages we hope you'll find the ideas you need for the life *you* want. Go on, help yourself.

It's what you make it

* * *

Change Your Life with NLP

The powerful way to make your whole life better

2nd edition

LINDSEY AGNESS

Prentice Hall Life
is an imprint of

Harlow, England • London • New York • Boston • San Francisco • Toronto • Sydney • Singapore • Hong Kong
Tokyo • Seoul • Taipei • New Delhi • Cape Town • Madrid • Mexico City • Amsterdam • Munich • Paris • Milan

PEARSON EDUCATION LIMITED
Edinburgh Gate
Harlow CM20 2JE
Tel: +44 (0)1279 623623
Fax: +44 (0)1279 431059
Website: www.pearsoned.co.uk

First published in Great Britain in 2008
Second edition 2011

Pearson Education is not responsible for the content of third party internet sites.

ISBN 978-0-273-73592-2

British Library Cataloguing-in-Publication Data
A catalogue record for this book is available from the British Library

Library of Congress Cataloging-in-Publication Data
Agness, Lindsey.
   Change your life with NLP : the powerful way to make your whole
   life better / Lindsey Agness. -- 2nd ed.
       p. cm.
   ISBN 978-0-273-73592-2 (pbk.)
  1.   Neurolinguistic programming.   2.   Success--Psychological aspects.
I. Title.
   BF637.N46A36 2011
   158.1--dc22
                                                    2010040368

10 9 8 7 6 5 4 3 2 1
14 13 12 11 10

Cartoon illustrations by Bill Piggins
Typeset in 9.5/13pt IowanOldBT by 30
Printed and bound in Great Britain by Henry Ling Ltd, Dorchester, Dorset

Thank you...

To my mother who taught me the benefit of learning to focus, work hard and achieve my dreams....

Endorsements from the first edition

'I would just like to say you really have shown me the light! I've been on NLP practs and yet after reading about you and then reading your book the lights went on! Bless you girl, if you can do that for me god knows what you can do!!!'

Bill, London

'I just felt compelled to drop you a note and tell you how incredibly engaging and accurate your writing is, very wise and inspiring words and now you've got me gripped. I've had some life-changing moments myself over the last 18 months and am well on my way and back on track to living my life with passion, purpose and positive intention.'

Kath, Birmingham

'Thank you again for your time and I would just like to say that I was so impressed not only with your wonderful book, but also the professionalism and ability in your "therapy". A very heartfelt "thank you".'

Nikki, Hampshire

'Your book on NLP really helped me a lot in my work as an academic ... I work for a very prestigious university in the UK and as a guest lecturer in others abroad. Indeed, I am using NLP to help my students ... not only that, I also use in my own personal life ... P.S. I have read other books on NLP, but yours was the best! Keep on!'

Alison, London

'I have been reading your book and I am up to Chapter 5. It is Fantastic. I love it.'

Geoff, Newcastle

'I just felt inspired and compelled to let Lindsey know how much I enjoyed her book ... I have read soooo many lifechanging/self-help

books and this is a really great one which I found very useful and resonated with me. The difference with this one is that I not only enjoyed it and could relate to it, but that I have started taking action straight away. Being a procrastinator, this has been an amazing shift.'

Fiona, Bristol

'I'm a 20-year-old Hungarian guy who is working and studying in Aberdeen, Scotland. I'm so glad that I found your book. It changed my life and the way I live it.'

Adam, Hungary

'Firstly, what a great book, it has certainly been an eye opener as this is my first encounter with NLP, all this and I haven't even finished it yet! I tell you, as I read this sometimes, I actually feel chills going up and down my spine as a result of the energy generated. Loving the book and looking forward to finishing it.'

Eyad, London

'I would like to say thank you to Lindsey, I have just finished reading her book and have not been able to put it down! From the first page I felt enriched by your words. The concepts were not new to me, but the honesty and clarity have delivered the content to me in a profound yet subtle and energising way. I know it works; it was not by accident that I picked up your book! I can now say that I have started my journey towards the Brilliant Zone!'

Laura-Marie, Suffolk

'I have just finished reading your book: Change Your Life with NLP and wanted to say thank you. The approach you shared gives an inspirational key for me to create a fulfilling and challenging career. I have been fortunate to receive a fantastic education and have enormous energy that I have been able to commit successfully to other goals in my life. Until now however I have not had the courage, techniques or discipline to apply myself to creating a career that I can be proud of. I am going to follow the approach you lay out, starting from today, and stick to it until I reach career goals that truly inspire me. Thank you for revealing this exciting new future.'

Adam, London

Contents

Foreword ix

About the author x

Introduction – could your life be better? xi

The ultimate test xiv

1 **What can NLP do for me?** 1

2 **Are you in the Grey Zone?** 9

3 **What would you do if you knew you couldn't fail?** 25

4 **Focus on what you want** 45

5 **Who am I?** 65

6 **Results or excuses? Taking responsibility for what you really want** 89

7 **Believe you can** 103

8 **You have all you need to succeed** 119

9 **Influencing with integrity** 143

10 **Step up with feedback** 169

11 **Get started** 181

12 **Do you want it or what?** 193

CONTENTS

My moment of truth 206

What next? 209

Reading and films list 211

Appendix 1: My meta programmes 213

Appendix 2: The language used by different representational
systems 219

Foreword

The first edition of this book was my own personal example of how you can use NLP to change your life. I was 47 when I wrote this book. It was my first. Motivated and excited at the potential I'd already found for NLP to change lives, I set upon the ambitious task of reaching far more people than I could ever hope to train! The book achieved more than I dared to dream about in assisting readers to pluck up the courage to take the first step towards their dreams.

It's not an NLP textbook in the traditional sense of the word, nor was it ever meant to be. So, if you already know a lot about NLP or you want a theoretical guide to NLP, this may not be the book for you. However, if you want to gain the basics of NLP and, most importantly, be able to apply the tools and techniques to make a difference in your life or the lives of others, then this book offers you a 'how to' guide with lots of practical exercises explained in terms that anyone can understand and then apply.

When I was asked for a second edition, I wondered what to add to widen the tools I could offer to you. Two new chapters emerged. The first, called 'Who am I?', uses NLP tools to show you who you are at your core. Self-awareness is the initial step towards personal leadership as you learn about your own personality. The second is called 'Influencing with Integrity', which shows you how to communicate more effectively and make more impact with others.

Enjoy the journey...

About the author

Lindsey Agness is a highly qualified and experienced NLP trainer, business consultant and owner of The Change Corporation. Lindsey uses her skills to train and coach both individuals and companies to transform themselves. She uses the techniques in this book on a daily basis, not only with her clients, but also on herself, to ensure that she is living the life she wants to live. She works with some of the biggest names in business as well as running many popular training seminars and motivational speaking assignments.

Introduction – could your life be better?

It doesn't matter how you have lived your life until this moment. All that matters is what your dreams are, what you ache for in the future. The only moment is **now**. Living in the past can slow us down as much as worrying about the future. Change can happen in an instant, in the blink of an eye or the click of a finger, once you have made a decision to go for it. Think about it – you start to create your future as soon as you make a decision.

I'm curious to know, could your life be better? Ask yourself the following questions to find out:

- Am I getting what I want out of life?   Yes / No
- Do I have stretching goals for the future?   Yes / No
- Am I reaching my full potential?   Yes / No
- Am I fulfilled by my work?   Yes / No
- Is my relationship the way I dreamed about?   Yes / No
- Do I have enough money to do what I want to do with my life?   Yes / No
- Is my life in balance?   Yes / No
- Am I happy with my body shape?   Yes / No
- Do I have enough energy to enjoy my day?   Yes / No

If you answered 'yes' to all the questions, you're probably reading the wrong book. Go off and enjoy your life! If, however, you answered 'no' to one or more of the questions, there is definitely potential for your life to be different – and so much better. You probably feel right now that your life is OK and yet you have a yearning for something else. Do you recognise this? Perhaps there is a dream you have always wanted to pursue or an area of your life that is not right yet. This is how I felt. I wanted to set up my own business...

I worked for many years as a coach and trainer for one of the world's largest consulting firms. I was helping business leaders across the world to make positive changes in their lives and their companies. Yet, I was still afraid to live my dream.

After a while I began to see strong patterns in how people changed. And I personally discovered that even making big changes can be much less scary than you think. The keys are:

- Find out what makes you truly happy – you will feel compelled to take action.
- Focus on what you want – you will be amazed at how quickly you attract these things to you.
- Adopt the right attitude so you see the benefits of all situations. Our lives are governed by how we react to events, not by what happens to us.
- See your life as an adventure and you will start to enjoy the journey.
- Keep going and keep learning along the way.

I decided to go for it myself. I put in place small steps to follow my dream and I was astonished at how good it felt. I started by doing freelance work part-time. Then I set up my company and left my job. At that moment I cannot explain how wonderful I felt because I had had the courage to make a decision and go for it. I knew that life would never be the same again.

It is that feeling I want you to experience.

It doesn't have to be setting up your own business. Maybe for you the dream will be about doing something you've always wanted to do, finding purpose and meaning in your life, improving or changing your relationship, moving to a new area or country, getting on top of your money issues, losing weight, finding another job – or all of these things!

What if your dreams were to become your reality? I want to inspire you to create new choices for your future and encourage you to take a chance and do something different. Whenever I start my training programmes, I always start with the story of my most important training prop. I show my students an elastic band which I wear constantly around my wrist and ask them why they think it's significant. What do you think? The answer is that an elastic band, once stretched, never quite goes back into the same place ever again. Once you learn something new, you can't unlearn it. If you read this book and do the exercises in it, I guarantee that you and your life will never be the same again.

Before we go any further, I have a question for you:

Are you prepared to step up to what you really want in life? To be the person you deserve to be? To do whatever it takes?

If you are, then please read on, and if not, then have a great life wondering what might have been.

The ultimate test

It's August and I'm on the firewalk instructors' Trainers' Training in Scotland with my trainer Peggy Dylan. It's already day three of the week-long training and I've slowly begun to get over my fears of walking on fire. The first night was a stretch. We made the fire as a group – that part was fun. Then we lit the fire and watched as the flames grow higher and higher, hotter and hotter. After a couple of hours, the wood had burned to coals and it was time to walk. I had never been so terrified of anything in my life. I had experienced some other powerful metaphors for change before – like the board break where you break a piece of pine with the energy and speed of your body. That had been amazing enough, yet this was on a different scale. The smoke from the heat of the fire made my eyes smart as I took my turn to rake the wood into the coal bed that we would later walk upon. I held back as my colleagues walked before me. When it was my turn the support and energy of the group literally 'willed' me over the hot coals. I was safe.

Tonight is different from the normal firewalk preparations. Peggy asks us to sit in a large circle and she arrives with a box which she proceeds to hand around the group. It feels rather like the game of 'pass the parcel' as we all pick a number and move the box on to the next person. I look at my number – 11 – about in the middle of the group. I'm very curious about what the numbers are all about. At 9 p.m., just when it's getting dark, Peggy calls the person with the number '1' to follow her. They disappear for about 10 minutes whilst the rest of us sit around chatting nervously. We wonder if it is some of test of our resolve. When number 1 returns, number 2 is immediately led out of the room. Number

1 is calm and in an almost meditative state. Of course, we start to ask them questions about what had happened. They are frustratingly sworn to secrecy. This makes me even more nervous about what is to come. I wait as numbers 1–10 leave the room and all of them return about 10 minutes later. They all seem very calm after their secret experience. Suddenly, number 10 is back and it is my turn. I follow Peggy out of the room rather tentatively. She explains that tonight a fire has been lit in the woods for each of us to have the experience of walking alone. She says that the decision to walk or not to walk is entirely our own, that we will learn something important whatever choice we make.

As I walk down to the fire alone, I am aware of an eerie silence – nothing like the high energy of the other evenings. I can hear the crickets and birds and the crackling of the fire as I walk through shrubbery and into the woods. It is a full moon and through the trees the flaming orange glow of the embers guide me down to the fire.

I stand at the foot of the fire and admire it for a while. It is a delight to all the senses. I can see the bright orange coals, hear the crackling of the fire, smell the oakiness of the burning wood, taste the smoke in the air and feel the anticipation of the opportunity to walk alone. It seems to me in that instant as I stand before the fire that everything I have achieved so far is nothing compared to this moment. To walk alone without the company and supportive energy of the group means everything. This moment symbolises whether or not I will do whatever it takes to achieve my dreams. Time is running away and I know that I only have a few more seconds to decide what I am going to do. I can literally hear my heart beating faster and faster in my chest. This is my moment of truth. Do I want it or what?

Chapter

1

'The science of excellence and the art of change'

What can NLP do for me?

This book is about improving your life, making the changes you want to make, using the techniques of NLP. Let's start with a quick look at what NLP actually is and where it came from. In the early 1970s, a linguist, John Grinder, and a mathematician, Richard Bandler, studied individuals who were excellent communicators and technicians of personal change.

The question they asked was, 'What is the difference between somebody who is merely competent and somebody who excels at the same skill?' The answers produced NLP: the science of excellence...the art of change.

They observed many world-class performers, including famous psychotherapists, and discovered the beliefs, mindset and strategies which delivered their success. They explored both personal and professional change work to discover tools and techniques that deliver fast and sustainable results. As a result, they formalised their change techniques under the name 'Neuro-Linguistic Programming', known as NLP, to symbolise the relationship between the brain, language and the body with the results that can be achieved. Because of these modelling techniques, NLP is often described as a kind of reverse engineering.

Unlike other approaches that tell you **what** you need to do, NLP is a **how to** technology. It tells and shows you **how to** be what you want to be, have what you want to have and do what you want to do. An intoxicating combination. This means it is possible to have the personal success you want right now. For most people things happen and they react. NLP offers a better way. It gives you tools to react differently by choice, to be more aware of your thoughts, feelings and behaviour. You are then ready to take responsibility for your results in all areas of your life.

NLP provides a set of tools and techniques to help you deal with unhelpful patterns of thought and behaviour. Although there are many techniques in NLP, you can make amazing changes by using just one technique. So imagine how much you will achieve by reading this book! Let's look at each part of NLP in turn and I'll explain what it's all about.

Neuro

Neuro is all about what we **think** – or our thoughts.

Neuro means 'what goes on inside our heads'. We have over 60,000 thoughts a day. These form our internal world of pictures, sounds and feelings. It is these conversations, dialogues or arguments we have with ourselves in our thinking process that drive how we feel, our mood and ultimately how we respond to events. In NLP terms, these are called our internal representations. For example, if you open your curtains on a miserable rainy day, you may, as a consequence, feel lousy, and this will drive how your day goes for you. Alternatively, you can open the curtains and think to yourself, 'It's a brilliantly rainy day today!' and go off and have fun. Another example would be if you are getting ready for an important night out – maybe with a potential new partner. You are excited and focused on the evening going well and how you will feel as a result. This will impact directly on the success of the evening.

The critical point to realise is that we can control our thoughts. This is very important because how we feel, how we behave and ultimately the results we get are driven by combinations of these internal representations which form our repeating patterns or habits. We run these patterns or habits over and over again unless they are interrupted or redirected. Sometimes these patterns serve us well but often they sabotage our potential success. The trick is to ensure that the 60,000 thoughts you have every day are good ones! Work out for yourself what proportion of your thoughts is helping you to achieve what you want and what proportion is in some way holding you back.

Linguistic

Linguistic is all about what we **say**, both verbally and non-verbally.

Language determines how we communicate with other people and ourselves. It is how we label our experiences and much more. Empowering language generates empowered behaviour. Likewise, negative language, such as excuses, is the result of disempowering thoughts and often happens without our realising it. It's negative language that limits our choices.

It is estimated that 93 per cent of communication is non-verbal. This means how you say what you say (intonation, volume, speed, etc.) carries five times more information than the words spoken. And how you use your body (gestures, facial expressions, posture) is even more influential. As our thoughts and feelings literally 'leak' out of us through our bodies, consider what yours say about you. Do they portray low self-esteem or someone who has confidence and knows what they want?

Programming

Programming is all about what we **do**.

We are all running programmes in our minds, all of the time. These programmes, patterns of behaviour and strategies drive the way we behave, our performance and ultimately our results. A phobia is a good example of how the brain works. A particular situation or trigger, such as flying, produces a strong physical response (sweaty palms, fast breathing, panic, etc.). The brain learns quickly and, thereafter, every time the person is presented with the same stimulus, their body knows to have the same response. The amazing thing is, people with phobias **never** forget to have this response. This is the perfect one-time learning strategy! Often, as with phobias, you run strategies that do not serve you – they even sabotage you. NLP teaches us how to change these ineffective strategies or programmes for ever.

To bring it altogether, NLP symbolises the relationship between the brain, language and the body. It describes how what we say, think and do interplay and affect our body, our behaviour and our results.

Applications of NLP

With NLP you can learn how to be in charge of your mental and physical state, create the perfect relationship, achieve success in your career and business, make more money, increase your motivation, boost your confidence and communicate effectively to produce the kind of results you want. One of the best things about NLP is that it has been designed to be learned easily and can be applied to any professional or personal situation.

NLP can help you to:

- change low self-esteem
- feel happier
- banish anxiety from your life
- get rid of bad habits
- lose weight and keep it off
- get out of debt
- work out what you want in all areas of life
- find the perfect partner or career
- communicate better
- learn faster
- reach peak performance in sport
- get messages across effectively.

Just imagine for a moment what NLP can do for you.

Experience the magic now

Here is a couple of quick exercises to help change how you feel in an instant.

Dealing with nerves

Do you have something coming up that you are nervous about? As you think about that situation now, looking through your own eyes, notice the pictures, sounds and feelings that are associated with that situation. Now imagine stepping backwards out of your body so you can see yourself, in front of you. As you look at yourself, notice how your feelings have already changed. Increase the distance between you and the picture of you in front and notice how you feel even more calm now.

How was that? Easy, wasn't it?

Dealing with procrastination

Do you ever procrastinate about a particular task or situation? We all do from time to time. As you think about something that you procrastinate about, do you have a picture? By picture, I don't mean a picture as clear as a photograph. I mean a sensation of that thought located in some direction in relation to your body. So, if I were to ask you where the picture is, to what direction would you point? You may notice it in front of you, to one side or behind you. Any location is perfect. Clear the screen and the picture. Now think of something you are totally motivated about. As you think about it, do you have a different picture? What is the location of that picture? Notice that it's different from the first picture. Clear the screen and the picture. Now here goes. Get back the picture of the situation you procrastinate about and move it into the same position as the thing you are totally motivated about. Notice what happens. You immediately feel more motivated to do the task you used to procrastinate about. That was easy too, wasn't it? I always use this technique to motivate myself when it's time to spring clean my cupboards at home!

These exercises demonstrate that NLP is fun and gets fast results – it provides an instruction manual for our brain.

How NLP is used in this book

In this book you will learn and apply many of the tools and techniques offered by NLP:

- understanding the secrets of success
- setting compelling goals that you are totally motivated to achieve
- understanding what motivates you
- focusing on what you want in order to attract it to you
- taking personal responsibility for the changes you want to create
- creating empowering beliefs about yourself
- changing your feelings and thoughts in an instant
- reframing old ideas
- taking control of your time
- maximising your personal energy and power
- utilising feedback to step up to the next level
- building your personal resilience
- learning from your experiences
- modelling the excellent results of others
- finally – totally going for it.

Many of these tools and techniques are from traditional NLP, others I've adapted for today's reality. I know this book will change your life. Are you ready for the ride?

Tip: If you always do what you've always done, you'll always get what you've always got! The message is clear: if what you're doing isn't working, do something different.

Chapter

2

'One can never consent to creep when one
feels an impulse to soar'

Helen Keller

Are you in the Grey Zone?

As a business consultant, I learnt that it was important to begin a new change project with a measurement or benchmark of how a company was performing at that moment. If you don't know where you're starting from it's harder to know where you've moved to. With that in mind, I invite you to complete the following quiz to find out if you're in the Awful, Grey or Brilliant zones. Be honest with yourself.

The Personal Discovery Quiz

1. When you wake up in the mornings, do you:
   a. Jump out of bed excited about the day that lies ahead?
   b. Have to drag yourself out from under the duvet?
   c. Feel exhausted as you've been unable to sleep well?
2. When your friend asks you how you are, do you answer:
   a. 'Absolutely brilliant'?
   b. 'Mustn't grumble'?
   c. 'Don't even ask'?
3. As you consider your goals for the future, do you:
   a. Feel really motivated?
   b. Think 'What goals?'?
   c. Go blank as you're struggling to get through today?
4. Your best friend asks you away for an exotic holiday. Do you:
   a. Say 'yes' immediately?
   b. Panic as you don't like going abroad?
   c. Say 'no' as you're too busy paying off all your debts right now?

5. When did you last spend time developing yourself?
   a. Within the past month.
   b. You can't remember.
   c. You think 'What's the point?'.

6. An opportunity for you to go for promotion comes up. Do you:
   a. Relish the challenge?
   b. Tell yourself you'll never get it?
   c. Behave like an ostrich as you can't be bothered even to think about it?

Add up the number of times you chose each letter, and then see below what the results suggest about you:

Highest score 'Cs' – I imagine that your life feels at rock bottom right now. When does it get bad enough for you to shift yourself out of the **Awful Zone**?

Highest score 'Bs' – even if you don't realise it yet, you are firmly in the **Grey Zone** and it's time to work out what you really want.

Highest score 'As' – congratulations! You are already moving in the direction of the **Brilliant Zone** where life is pretty amazing, and I'll show you how it can get even better.

The Awful Zone

“By changing what we link pain and pleasure to we will instantly change our behaviour.”
                                                    Tony Robbins

People move into the Awful Zone most frequently when a life-changing event occurs that leads to the equilibrium and malaise of the Grey Zone being disturbed. For example, the death of a loved one, the onset of a life-threatening illness, divorce and so on.

Why is it that some people can experience pain and still fail to change? In my experience it's because they haven't experienced enough pain yet. Every one of us has a threshold for pain and once that threshold is crossed, change will occur. The threshold is different for everyone. That is why two soldiers returning from active service may respond differently to their experiences; one may get on with their life as if nothing has happened and the other may suffer from post-traumatic stress disorder. The Awful Zone is the point of no return. This is the place where the pain gets so great that you finally take action. At this point, although it is bizarre to describe it as such, the pain does you a favour as it drives you to take action and produce different results. This is the terrain of the Awful Zone.

Kay – facing the most challenging circumstances of her life

Kay had worked in local government for 20 years. She was a third-tier manager in a busy social services department in London. She decided not to go for promotion to the vacant assistant director post when the opportunity arose as she had recently had her son. Her new boss was incompetent at his job and lazy. This had a 'double whammy' effect on her as he over-delegated and she had to pick up the pieces when he didn't do his job properly. She soon became extremely unhappy. She was in the Grey Zone as she had worked for this organisation for the whole of her working life and she knew nothing else. Yet, she was too afraid to move into something new.

Then a life-changing experience occurred that tipped her into the Awful Zone. Her brother-in-law, who was in his mid-forties, was diagnosed with an inoperable brain tumour. He had been married to her sister for 20 years and although they had always thought they would have children, they had come to terms with the fact that it was unlikely to happen now. Imagine how happy they were when his wife discovered she was pregnant. This was five months before her husband's diagnosis. The pregnancy became fraught with the expectation of new life and loss of life at the same time. In the end, he deteriorated fast and died a week after his daughter was born. It was as if he held on long enough to hold his new daughter in his arms and then it was time.

The significance of this experience for Kay was life changing: being with her sister and her brother-in-law throughout these tragic circumstances was her tipping point. She decided to take action at work and took the matter up formally. Despite her loyalty of service and her well-known ability to deliver results, the Authority failed to deal with the situation. She decided that life was too short to spend any more time in a job that caused so much unhappiness and she finally left.

She decided to set up her own company where she would be the controller of her own universe and her life began to improve immediately.

One of the important questions for you is, 'when is the pain bad enough?' Do you want to find yourself looking back on your life full of regret? The great thing is that it's never too late to change.

The Grey Zone

"People often end up feeling that their lives have been wasted, that instead of being filled with happiness their years were spent in anxiety and boredom." **Mihaly Csikszentmihalyi**

I describe the Grey Zone as that place where many people spend their entire lives – it's not awful and it's certainly not brilliant. It's OK and it's the place where people are prepared to sell out on their dreams for a comfortable existence. **What a waste of a life!** Often people are happy in the Grey Zone but that's because they don't know any other way of living. Over the years spent coaching and training many people, I have realised that most of the population settle for second best because they haven't got the courage to do anything about changing their situation. There's a saying: 'If you always do what you've always done you always get what you've always got.' That's the mantra of those who live their lives in the Grey Zone. Life in the Grey Zone feels familiar, comfortable, unfulfilling and **stuck**, and those in the Grey Zone do not feel they have any choice but to remain where they are.

Over the years I have also been given many excuses (sorry, reasons!) by my clients for staying in the Grey Zone. Here are the most common ones:

'I'm not good enough to get what I really want.'

'I can't risk giving up a good salary.'

'I won't get another job very easily.'

'It's too late for me to change now.'

'No one will listen to me.'

'It's better to stay with my partner rather than be on my own.'

Do these sound familiar to you? Be honest with yourself.

Paul – putting responsibility above happiness and fulfilment

I met an old friend recently who had just retired after spending his whole life in the insurance business. As I congratulated him on the 40 years he had spent dedicating his life to the same company, I noticed him hesitate slightly as he looked away for a moment. When his eyes returned my gaze, I saw what could only be described as a look of disappointment as he told me that he had never intended to stay in his job for so long. It had been his father who had encouraged him to go into the insurance business in the beginning as it was seen as a 'steady' job. He, on the other hand, had never enjoyed the sales part of his role as he was quite a shy and reserved person. I wondered why he had never pursued a job that suited him more and I asked him what had prevented him from changing careers once he discovered that insurance was not for him. He shifted around uncomfortably on the spot before telling me that he had had too many responsibilities in his life to be able to do what he really wanted to do for himself. I asked him if he had told his family about how he truly felt about his insurance job. He replied that he had kept his dreams to himself and had gone about his work as cheerfully as possible over the years. I felt a sense of loss and waste on his behalf as I walked off down the road.

Paul had spent his career firmly in the Grey Zone. Can you imagine what that would be like? I'm wondering to what extent your job is helping you to achieve your potential. Do you wake up in the mornings full of energy and eager to get started, or do you want to turn over, wrap yourself in the duvet and groan? Are you heading towards a similar experience as Paul? Be honest with yourself.

The Brilliant Zone

"Every day brings a chance for you to draw in a breath, kick off your shoes, and dance.**"**
                                                            Oprah Winfrey

The Brilliant Zone is the caretaker of our dreams. You know if you are heading in the direction of the Brilliant Zone because it feels exciting, motivating, exhilarating and stretching. These are our moments of **optimal experience**. In my experience, the journey towards the Brilliant Zone is not about the passive, receptive, relaxing times, although such experiences are great if we have worked hard to attain them. Instead, the best moments are when our bodies and/or our minds are stretched to their limits to achieve something difficult and worthwhile. The difference is that these are the experiences we **make** happen.

Those with courage move out of the Grey Zone and towards the Brilliant Zone. And, anyone can achieve this. In fact, it's already too late for you because now you know that the Brilliant Zone exists and that it's possible to get there. What makes the difference? Those that move outside are the people with a **compelling** dream for the future. They are totally focused on their dream and failing is not an option. They never say 'I can't'. Instead they say 'Why not!' You can probably think of a number of successful people who have this philosophy in life.

Can you or can't you?

Virgin boss, Richard Branson, doesn't believe that a little word like 'can't' should stop you. He had a great teacher. His mother wanted to be a pilot during the war and was told that only men could be pilots. Despite being very attractive, she wore a leather flying jacket and hid her blond hair under a leather helmet. She practised speaking with a deep voice and got the job she wanted. After the war, she wanted to be an air hostess. For this you had to speak Spanish and be trained as a nurse. Branson's mum chatted up the night porter at the airline and he secretly put her name on the list. Soon after she was an air hostess. She still couldn't speak Spanish and she wasn't a nurse but she had used her determination and her courage. When Branson was only four years of age, his mother used to stop the car a few miles from their house and tell her son to find his own way home across the fields. She made it a game, albeit one that would be unlikely these days, and he was happy to play along. It was an early challenge for him. As he grew older, the challenges grew harder. His mother always drove him to want to do his best and to chase his dreams. Branson says that hard work and fun were family traits.

I spent many years in the Grey Zone, although it might have looked to others as if I had the perfect job. The job wasn't awful – in fact it was well paid and I got to travel round the world. But, it still wasn't my dream. The hours were long and the increasing time away from home meant that I was apart most weeks from my young family and husband. I felt out of control. I was firmly stuck in the Grey Zone.

Then, in 1997, something happened that was to change my whole life and begin to move me towards the Brilliant Zone. I did my first NLP training course. It completely blew me away. At the end of the course I had goals for the first time in my life, I felt motivated, believed I had choices and I wanted to discover what I was really capable of achieving.

Once you learn something you can't unlearn it

I knew that my life and my model of the world would never be the same again. On my return to work I began to develop my dream of having my own company and I worked on a strategy to get funding to do my next NLP training. That's one thing you learn early on in NLP – that the most successful people always have the next goal in mind. The following year I did my Master Practitioner training and later my Trainer's training. Now everything was in place.

One of the reasons why people are comfortable in the Grey Zone is that they don't know that the Brilliant Zone exists because they've never been there. I knew by the end of my Trainer's training that the Brilliant Zone existed. It was too late for me to unlearn it and I was determined to get there and stay there. The excitement that I experienced as I began to develop my plan for my business was like nothing I'd ever experienced before. I felt alive for the first time in years – maybe for the first time in my adult life. I enjoyed waking up and going to work as each day took me closer to my goal. Every day I asked myself what I had achieved that day to take me closer to my goal.

Acting 'as if'

I wondered how I would ever know enough to run my own business. Through my NLP training I came across 'Heisenberg's principle'. This states that 100 per cent certainty doesn't exist. Successful people take risks because they accept that they will never know everything they need to know. But they act 'as if' they do know and take the plunge. The journey is exciting – that's the thing. That's what it's going to be like for you too as you move towards the Brilliant Zone.

Rebecca – living the life of her dreams

Out of all of my clients over the years, Rebecca knew exactly what she wanted. She set a goal to run her own business and to start a new relationship. Her goal was to set up her own graphic design company. However, she knew very little about business. She modelled a number of very successful businesspeople to discover what made their businesses a success. She traded her design skills for some of their valuable time and experience. Her vision and focus were so clear that she quickly began to bring in clients. Three years on, she now runs a well-known brand consultancy business that works with top corporations. As for the new relationship, she set aside part of her wardrobe for her future partner's clothes and began to sleep on 'her' side of the bed in anticipation. She attracted a man who adores her and assists her to develop her company as well. They were married recently.

The exercises

The exercises are a *vital part* of this book. They are designed specifically to help you integrate everything you will learn easily. I encourage you to complete them as fully as possible as they will literally move you to the next level. You can complete them in the book or, if you prefer, copy them into a personal notebook or journal. This and subsequent chapters have a number of critical exercises to reinforce the learning.

There are three ways that people learn. Firstly, you may find yourself enjoying reading this book and using the exercises to make new discoveries about yourself. It's a pleasurable adventure. You relish the new opportunities to change your life as you gain momentum and confidence with each chapter. That's the best way to experience this journey.

Secondly, you may feel some resistance to what you learn about yourself. You may feel uncomfortable at times as you become more and more honest with yourself about where you are and how you really feel about that. Good! When you feel resistance, you know that you are on the verge of a great learning opportunity. It's even more important in these moments to stay with the exercises and to get the learnings for yourself. It will be in one of these specific moments that you discover the most important personal message to you from this book.

Thirdly, you may even feel pain as you discover how stuck you have been in your past life – whether it's your job, relationship or your health and fitness that has suffered. In these moments you have the opportunity to take action and to begin your journey. I will assist you, and I congratulate you for having the guts to face up to whatever is going on. These are moments of decision for you when you have the opportunity to change your future. It doesn't have to be the same as it has been – you always have a choice. Remember that.

Exercise 1

Where am I on the grid of life?

As you read about the three zones and the stories of the people in them, I'm wondering where you are right now? Do you want to find out? Are you ready to find out? Breathe, find a pen and take the first step of your journey towards the Brilliant Zone.

Bearing in mind your answers to the quiz at the start of this chapter, mark where you believe you are on the grid of life (see diagram). Be honest with yourself. Are you closer to the Awful Zone or the Brilliant Zone?

As you look at the grid, are you surprised about where you ended up? Now you are more consciously aware of what your life is like, let's consider how you can begin to take the first step towards the Brilliant Zone.

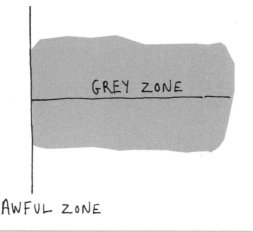

BRILLIANT ZONE

GREY ZONE

AWFUL ZONE

How do you move out of the Grey Zone?

Why do people stay in the Grey Zone? In the examples I've discussed, the same reason kept everyone in the Grey Zone – **fear**. We are scared of moving into the unknown, of doing something different. Fear comes from limiting beliefs that we have about ourselves and our abilities. In fact, the consequences of our making a change are often built up in our minds to mean something far worse than the actual reality of the situation. Here's a great acronym for fear:

False

Evidence

Appearing

Real

Our minds are brilliant at creating the worst case scenario in our heads, and then that's what we begin to focus on as our reality. Soon we forget that it's not true. We make huge assumptions about what may or may not be true based upon our belief systems. And guess what? Our beliefs are generalisations passed on to us by those who influenced us in our early years. They are **not real**. The reality is very different if we are prepared to find out and start the journey.

It takes one of two things to move people out of the Grey Zone. Either you have a goal that is so compelling you will take the risk of going for it. Or, in contrast, the pain becomes so great that you are finally tipped over the edge of change.

Which one influences us often depends upon the way we are motivated. In NLP we talk about people being 'towards' or 'away from' motivated. Think about it. Do you move away from what you don't want or move towards what you do want? Are you a 'stick' or a 'carrot' person? For example, if you want to lose weight, do you move towards a goal of being fit and healthy and have a motivational image in your mind of you in that skimpy new outfit, or do you move away from being fat and focus on an image of you overweight and bulging out of that special outfit?

Sticking to your resolutions

One of the limitations of 'away from' motivation is that it often dwindles once short-term improvements are gained. For example, a lot of people's new year's resolutions (although they might not realise it) are about getting out of the Grey Zone or even the Awful Zone. They start off well, take action and before too long are moving in the right direction. As they begin to notice improvements in their life, they become comfortable again. As if by magic, their motivation vaporises and their action dwindles to nothing. In fact, the worst case scenario is that they begin to drift back towards the Awful Zone when the pain begins to increase again. This is the reason why so many diets do not work, because as soon as your target weight is reached, you feel comfortable again and are tempted to slip back into old habits. The alternative is to move towards a healthy lifestyle where taking exercise becomes part of a way of life.

Exercise 2

Am I 'towards' or 'away from' motivated?

Ask yourself the following question and write down your answers below:

'What do I want in my life?'

- ....
  ....

- ....
  ....

- ....
  ....

- ....
  ....

- ....
  ....

Notice how many of your answers start with what you don't want as opposed to what you do want. If the majority of your answers focus on what you don't want, you are more 'away from' motivated. For example, 'I don't want to be poor' is an example of an 'away from' motivated goal.' If your answers focus more on what you do want, you are more 'towards' motivated. For example, 'I want abundance in my life' is an example of a 'towards' motivated goal.' Or you might have said something like 'I don't want to be bored' (away from) as opposed to 'I want the opportunity to travel' (towards).

Now consider what it would take for you to move out of the Grey Zone and write your answer below:

Notice again whether you are 'towards' or 'away from' motivated.

Now write down honestly what has prevented you from moving out of the Grey Zone so far:

The good news is that you always have other choices even if it doesn't seem that way right now. If you don't believe that you have other choices at the moment, I want you to pretend that it's true, especially as you complete Exercise 3, overleaf. I believe that my job is about giving other people more choices about what they can achieve in their lives.

Exercise 3

What would I do if I knew I couldn't fail?

I want you to dream for a moment. Think about what you would change in your life if I guaranteed that you couldn't fail. Anything in your life at all. Write your answers below:

- ....
  ....
- ....
  ....
- ....
  ....
- ....
  ....
- ....
  ....
- ....
  ....
- ....
  ....

Now take another look at your list and make sure that you have really stretched yourself. This is the moment that you can dream.

Really enjoy the anticipation of achieving these things in future as you move on to the next chapter.

Tip: If you're still reluctant to move out of the Grey Zone, imagine turning the clock forward 10 years and you still haven't got what you really want and you're 10 years older. How frustrating would that be? Take the first step. You know you want to.

Chapter

3

'People are not lazy. They simply have impotent goals
– that is goals that do not inspire them.'

Tony Robbins

What would you do if you knew you couldn't fail?

Why dream?

Thomas Edison is a great example of a man focused on a dream. He was one of the most prolific inventors of our time. Edison is best known for inventing the light bulb, which was patented in 1880. What really interests me though was his focus and determination to achieve his dream. Fortunately for us he didn't give up his dream after the first few failed attempts to invent the light bulb. In the period from 1878 to 1880 Edison and his associates worked on at least 3,000 different theories to develop an efficient incandescent lamp. Each failed attempt he believed to be a step closer to the solution. For him it was just feedback about how not to do it next time. His dream has impacted on every household from that moment on. One of the most inspiring quotes that I have come across over the years and use regularly in my training room is by Edison:

> **"**I am not discouraged, because every wrong attempt discarded is another step forward.**"**

I often reflect on this when my ideas don't entirely go to plan.

I'm very curious about how you ended the last chapter. What were the things that you said you would do if you knew you couldn't fail? I suggest that you view these as your personal dreams. Were you surprised by some of the things you wrote?

Karen – a blooming future

A client of mine did not feel totally fulfilled in her job and was becoming more and more restless. She asked me to assist her to discover what she really wanted. She was surprised, when asked what she would do if she couldn't fail, to hear herself say the words 'open a florist shop'. She has since gone part-time in her old job and works every weekend at a successful florist in London learning the trade.

What if your dreams were to become your goals for the future? Goethe said that a dream is a forefeeling of something that will happen. I believe that any dream can become a goal when you have a plan and you take action. What's the purpose of a dream anyway if we never take any action? We stay in the Grey Zone always wondering what might have been. Instead, ask yourself what your stretching goals are for the future. I mean really stretching goals. Remember the elastic band.

Plato once said that the beginning is the most important part of any work. That's where having goals comes in. Research suggests that the ability of people to tap into their personal power is directly affected by their goals. This is the power of goal setting.

What is a goal?

"If a man knows not what harbour he seeks, any wind is the right wind.**"**   Seneca

A goal is something you want, something that is very important to you. The first rule of achieving your goal is that it must be compelling for you. You have to know why your goal is important to you or else you will not be motivated to really go for it. Be careful because if you set personal goals that you don't really want to achieve, perhaps because they're someone else's goals, you may end up with a life you don't want. I've coached a lot of people who have been surprised when they discover that they've been living their parents' or their partner's goal for themselves. In fact, I was one of them. In *The 7 Habits of Highly Effective People*, Stephen Covey likens this to leaning your ladder against the wrong wall. So you might strive for years to achieve a goal, gradually progressing up the ladder. But when you eventually get to the top and look around, you suddenly realise that you're in a place you never really wanted to get to.

You may even notice at this point that your life has been about supporting other people's goals. It's not uncommon for women in particular to focus their energies on supporting their children's or their partner's goals. The problem is when you turn around one day and your children have grown up and left home or your partner has moved on and you are left with emptiness where your future should be. Now it's time to consider what you really want for yourself.

My mother always taught me the importance of a good education and career. I thank her for that. She used to say to me that I had the opportunity to experience what she had missed out on. She still tells the stories of having to drag me out of my bedroom to stop doing school work and to come downstairs and watch the TV for a while before going to bed. I loved doing well at school because that's when I got the most attention from my parents. My mother is a very bright woman. She was the first in the family to go to the local grammar school and she excelled in all her exams. She desperately wanted to go to university but was unable to do so as my grandparents didn't have the funds to support her. Instead she went to secretarial college which guaranteed her a life of supporting others. My father was a motor mechanic and my mother always had big goals for him. He, however, is a reliable and unassuming man and was content to stay in the background quietly supporting his family. He never shared her ambition for him to run his own garage. After many years of disappointment, my mother turned her attentions to me. I don't think she ever did it consciously but her attitude and behaviour towards me had an enormous impact on my early life as I was the one singled out to live out the life she had never been able to experience. This has always been an important driving force in my life and has given me focus and determination and I thank her for that.

She was so proud when I was poached from my job in local government to be offered a role as change management consultant at one of the top global consulting firms. Whereas she'd been the first to go to grammar school, I was the first person in my family to have broken the mould of the normal round of working-class opportunities. It was a great job. I was often embarrassed to hear my mother boasting to her friends about my latest successes. If they had an offspring about the same age as me who was not doing as well, all the better!

Yet, as I said earlier, something was missing for me. All finally became clear when, through NLP, I learned about values. Our values are what is really important to us. They drive our motivation and what we choose to do and how we evaluate ourselves after an event. If our values are not satisfied in a key area of our lives, we are likely to feel under stress and unhappy. Problems in relationships are often caused by a clash of values. Imagine in a relationship if one partner values spontaneity whilst the other values routine: there will come a time when there is a fundamental clash. In the beginning, a clash of values is less obvious as both partners make allowances and are more flexible than usual. However, once the dust has settled values will play a key role in whether the relationship survives long term. Similarly, with our careers, if our values are not being satisfied, we will feel under stress, unfulfilled and so on.

I discovered that I had values around independence, innovation, risk taking and significance – and that meant I would never be completely fulfilled in my old role.

The fastest way to find out your own values in any area of your life is to ask yourself a simple question. For example, if you want to know about your relationship values, ask yourself: 'What's most important to me about my relationship?'

This should be your ideal relationship, not the way it is at the moment. You then brainstorm with yourself or, even better, ask someone else to work with you on this. You just keep asking yourself the same question. Once you have run out of ideas, list them in priority order – you may be very surprised about what comes up. You can do this for any area of your life (see The Wheel of Life on page 32 for other ideas). We'll learn more about our values in Chapter 5.

The moral is that when setting personal goals, it's vital to choose a goal that you have a burning desire to achieve for **yourself**, that meets your personal values. Napoleon Hill talks about this in his classic book *Think and Grow Rich*. Although the goal on which the book focuses is making money, the principle applies equally to achieving any other sort of goal. Napoleon Hill says the first step towards riches is **desire**. Whatever goal you choose, make sure that you have a burning desire to achieve it.

How do you set goals?

As well as needing to be compelling, a goal is best stated simply and according to the principles of the ubiquitous SMART objectives. These principles were originally taken from Paul J. Meyer's book *Attitude is Everything*. They are not traditional NLP principles but I use them as they are the best way I have found to set up goals in a way that means they are easier to achieve.

- **Specific** – goals should be straightforward and emphasise what you want to happen. Specifics help you to focus your efforts and clearly define what you are going to do. For example, instead of setting a goal to lose weight or be healthier, set a specific goal to lose two centimetres off your waistline or to walk five miles a day.

- **Measurable** – if you can't measure it, you can't manage it. Choose a goal with measurable progress, so you can see the change occur. For example, 'I want to write one chapter a day for my book' shows the specific target to be measured.

- **Achievable** – all your goals should be achievable, which means they should be within the bounds of possibility for you. For example, it is within the bounds of possibility that I can win the London Marathon this year. That is because I have two legs, I can run and I enjoy training. In NLP we say that the 'A' also stands for 'Acting as if', the theory being that we will never know all we need to know. If we begin to 'act as if', our minds believe it to be real – that's why visualisation is very powerful in sports coaching.

- **Realistic** – this provides the check on achievable. It may be possible for me to win the London Marathon but is it realistic? Realistic, in this case, means 'do-able.' It means that the learning curve is not a vertical slope; that the skills needed to do the work are available. Set the bar high enough to find out what you are capable of but not so high that you will frustrate yourself when you never get there. Remember the elastic band. Focus on the inspirational, not the sensible!

- **Timed** – set a clear time frame for the goal: for next week, in three months, a year, five years, etc. Whatever fits with your goal. Putting an end point on your goal gives you a clear target to work towards. If you don't set a time, the commitment is too vague. It tends not to happen because you feel you can start at any time. Without a time limit, there's no urgency to start taking action now.

Your Wheel of Life

If you are not sure yet about the goals you want to focus on, use the Wheel of Life opposite to identify the areas of your life that are currently out of balance. The wheel contains the key areas of our lives – *career, family, relationships, personal development, health and fitness,* and *wealth.* These areas need to be in balance to achieve harmony and success. If one or more areas are out of balance, we are likely to be in the Grey Zone and suffering some stress.

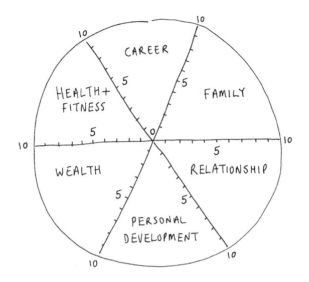

Exercise 4

My wheel of life

Consider your own life in relation to the six areas on the wheel above. If there's another area of life that is relevant to you and not shown then add it. Score each area out of 10 using the scale provided and add a mark against the score you have picked. You should score each area of life in turn. Once you have done this, join up all the 'marks' in order to discover the shape of your wheel.

Ask yourself:

- Which was my area of life with the lowest score?
- Which was my area of life with the highest score?
- Would my wheel travel smoothly on the ground or would there be bumps in the journey?
- Which area/s do I want to work on to develop my goals? (These would normally be the one or two areas with the lowest scores.)

Setting your own personal goals

Now it's your turn to develop your own personal goals. Remember the elastic band and stretch yourself. Be greedy as you think about your goals. What's the goal that will have the biggest impact on your life? Find somewhere quiet to relax and consider your goal. Think back to a time in the past when you did achieve your goal – whatever it was. Associate yourself back into that memory and remember how good it felt to be successful. Now double the feelings as you go into the next exercise to set your personal goals. If you haven't already got a goal in mind, then review the areas of your life with the lowest scores and the things you would change if you knew you couldn't fail from the end of Chapter 2. Now imagine turning the clock forward three years. What will you have achieved by then? What will you look like, sound like, feel like? What will others say about you? As you consider yourself and your successes, develop the most important goal you want to achieve. Make sure it's a SMART goal. If your goal is over a different timescale, then imagine turning the clock forward over the desired period of time. You can use the same process over and over again for other goals that you have.

Use present-tense language for your goals. It's important to behave as if you already have your goal as this gives your nervous system the impression that it's real. Your brain doesn't actually know the difference between what's real and what's imagined. I mentioned 'acting as if' in the section about SMART. It is one of the most important distinctions between successful people and those that never quite make it. Your brain cannot tell the difference and the new behaviours produce new neural pathways that reinforce the new behaviours. In fact, if you 'do' a new behaviour for at least 30 days consciously, it becomes an unconscious habit. For example, if you want to be promoted, you can act as if you already have been promoted and are doing the job above yours and see what happens. The only time I advise against acting as if is when your goal is to have £1 million in your bank account within a certain period of time and you start spending now!

One last check before you write anything down. Ask yourself what it is you want so much that it brings a huge smile to your face just thinking about it. Michael Neill said that the number one reason that people don't already have what they want is that they have learned not to let themselves want what they don't think they can have. In order to avoid disappointment, they shut off from wanting the dream and focus on what is realistic. Our friends and families can be our worst enemies when we aspire to what we really want. They ask us who we think we are. Or they are threatened by us actually doing something with our lives whilst they remain in the Grey Zone. Make sure that you focus on the inspirational rather than the sensible as you develop your goals and find out what you are truly capable of achieving.

Dave – transforming his life with powerful goals

Dave had inherited his father's carpet cleaning company. That was 25 years ago. It wasn't his ideal job yet it paid the mortgage and provided his family with a good standard of living. Two years ago he read his first personal development book, rather like this one, and began to understand that he could make different choices. He realised that he had become his own biggest barrier to change. He read all the books he could find. His dream was to be able to work as a life coach. His family and friends thought he was mad. He set his goal to become a successful coach earning double his salary from the carpet cleaning company in his first year. After training he was given the opportunity to work as a coach and hypnotherapist in a local clinic. He kept on the carpet cleaning business and asked one of his sons to take over as manager. He achieved all his goals and wondered why he had left it so long to move on.

Exercise 5

My goals

You'll notice that this exercise is set up for you to work out the final step in three years' time and then work backwards from that. If your goal is more long term or short term than this, adjust the stages accordingly.

Here is an example plan which is based on the following goal: 'To write a successful book that is accepted by a publisher with global reach, and which sells over 100,000 copies within three years'.

Three years

Revise and publish a new edition after selling 100,000 copies worldwide.

Two years

Sell over 40,000 copies in the UK alone and be on at least two bestseller listings. Book is translated into at least two other languages and is selling in all major countries worldwide.

Eighteen months

Launch book with excellent reviews in at least three magazines or newspapers. Achieve a minimum of three radio and TV interviews.

Within one year

Secure a contract with a well-known global publisher and write the first draft of the manuscript.

Within six months

Write the book proposal and find a publishing agent.

Within three months

Research the market and check that the topic is likely to sell. Learn how to write a book proposal in the quest to find an agent and publisher.

Within one month

Decide what the book will be about.

Now write your goals below:

Within three years

Within two years

Within 18 months

Within one year

Within six months

Within three months

Within one month

Before you move on, take another look at your goals and ask yourself if you've really stretched yourself enough.

Questioning for achievable outcomes

If I were to ask you whether you've ever had a goal in the past that you've achieved, I've got a feeling you'd say 'yes'. And, if I asked you whether you've ever had a goal in the past that you've not achieved, I've got a feeling that you'd also say 'yes'. I'm curious to know what makes the difference between the two goals. Maybe motivation was an issue for you if your goal was not compelling enough. I'm also curious to know why you haven't already achieved the goal that you've just written about. What if I could give you a tool that would guarantee you achieving your goal. Would that be useful to you?

The tool is a set of questions called 'Questioning for Achievable Outcomes', here used with permission (© The Tad James Co, Tad and Adriana James). I have shortened the list for practical purposes.

It's best to find a partner for this exercise so you can tell them out loud the answers to the questions. If that's not possible you can answer the questions yourself and write down the answers that you come up with. It is very important to write the answers down because once you commit the details of your goal to paper it becomes much more real.

Exercise 6

Questioning for achievable outcomes

It takes about 25 minutes to go through the exercise. Get your partner to ask the questions clearly and to assist you through the process as fast as possible. Ask your partner to write down your answers and give them to you after the exercise.

1. *What specifically do you want?* (Checks that your goal is stated clearly.)

2. *For what purpose do you want this goal?* (Checks that your goal is compelling to you.)

3. *Where are you now in relation to your goal?* (Checks the potential length of the journey. Are you close to success or are you at the very start?)

---

4. *What will you see/hear/feel when you have it?* (Creates a multi-sensory description that makes the goal more real.)

5. *How will you know when you have it?* (Checks your evidence criteria.)

6. *What do you have now and what do you need to achieve your outcome?* (Checks the resources you require to achieve the goal.)

7. *What will you gain or lose if you have it?* (Checks the impact of your goal on other areas of your life.)

What did you notice happening to your goal as you went through that process? Most people find that their goals become much clearer and they feel more committed towards them. The sensory description (i.e. what you see/hear/feel when you have it) really attaches you to your goal.

The impact question (number 7) is also very interesting because it flushes out what is called 'secondary gain' in NLP. It asks you to think about what you will lose as well as gain when you achieve your goal. For example, taking that job secondment to the US might be great for your career but will give you less time for your relationship and your children. It's very important that consequences are acknowledged and addressed because any internal conflict can cause you to give less than 100 per cent commitment to your goal, and you may end up compromising or even sabotaging your own success.

For example, secondary gain for me when I started my own company was the loss of my regular and generous salary. That kept me stuck in the Grey Zone for a long time. In fact, it took me three years to make the decision to leave my job and focus full-time on my company. So be honest with yourself about what you might lose, and later we'll deal with the fear of giving up those things to pursue your dreams.

Letting the specifics go

I don't believe that it's necessary to work out detailed plans to achieve each step along the journey towards achieving your goal. Mike Dooley, author and collaborator on the film *The Secret*, calls them 'the dreaded HOWs'. That might sound rather controversial for some people. I say this because there are a million ways in which you can achieve your goal. If you focus too rigidly on a particular path, you will not notice other possibilities that may come your way. If we focus on only one solution, then we miss the opportunity to spot whatever is not that one solution – that is everything else or infinite opportunities. Why would you want to constrain yourself when you can achieve your goal in many different ways?

For example, if you want to have a new relationship in your life, you may choose to focus all your energies on internet dating. Every evening and weekend you spend all your spare time checking any new dating prospects that have come online. Whilst you do that you are turning down regular opportunities to go out with your friends where you might also meet that special person. I'm not saying that you shouldn't go on to the web – I am saying that you should leave yourself open to all the other ways of meeting someone new as well.

Face the right way

The important thing is to set your attention in the right direction. Your energy then flows where your attention goes. Therefore, if you turn your attention to your goal and begin to take action, then success will follow. Leave the delivery to your unconscious mind and enjoy the journey. Just allow it to happen. You'll be astonished at how quickly you begin to attract to yourself people, places and things that will help you to achieve your goal.

Relax

It is also important to let go of it not being OK for you to not get your goal. This may sound contradictory to what I said earlier about your goal being compelling. However, if it's not OK for you to not get your goal you will focus on your anxieties about not getting the goal. If you focus on and place your attention on what you don't want (see Chapter 4), you are likely to attract exactly that thing to you. How do you avoid doing this? One way is to consider the worst thing that might happen if you don't get your goal – but only for as long as it takes for you to be OK with that and to let it go. For example, I considered what would be the worst thing that could happen if I didn't get my goal of running a successful company. For me that would mean that I would need to go back into paid employment and that felt fine. I then put the concept out of my mind and focused all my energy on the success of my company.

Keep going

John Grinder, the co-creator of NLP, said that in his experience the single key factor which stops people achieving their goal is that they don't have a goal beyond a goal. If there's nothing to aim for next, they can become demotivated and even sabotage themselves. For example, let's suppose my goal is to climb a mountain and I train really hard for it over a long period of time. If, when I reach the peak of the mountain, I am not already looking out at the next highest peak I may become demotivated. I may even begin to slide back into the Grey Zone because I have lost focus and direction in my life. So it's very important to enjoy the journey and always be aware of what comes next.

Responsibility for goals

I actually left my well-paid comfortable job twice. The first time was when a friend of mine had asked me to become her business partner and fellow director of her NLP training company. I was thrilled about this because although I'd wanted to set up my own business for at least two years I hadn't had the courage to go out completely on my own. Her company was already successful and making very good profits. However, after a very short period of time things began to go wrong. I couldn't understand this as I believed that I was focusing on my goal to have my own NLP training company and I had taken massive action towards that goal. Then one day something happened which had a profound effect on me. I had written a proposal for a potential new client and given it to our office manager to submit. Unknown to me, she gave it to my partner and it came back later covered in red pen as she disagreed with many of my ideas. I felt angry and hurt and suddenly it dawned on me that I was dancing to her tune, pursuing her dream and not my own. It was one of those light-bulb moments when I realised that I would not be happy until I was free to be true to my own goals and aspirations. I left soon afterwards and actually went back to my old employer for a while, rather bruised by the experience. I had seen her offer to me as a shortcut to having my own successful company. It seemed ideal and yet I was always likely to have to sell out on my own dreams in that situation.

These were powerful learnings for me. One of the principles of NLP is that 'there is no failure – only feedback', and I found this to be very motivating in this situation. I focused on my learnings from this experience, which should always be for the future and for yourself and be positive.

My learnings were as follows.

- When you take 100 per cent responsibility for achieving your outcome and are willing to do it all by yourself, you won't have to.

- To the extent that you are not willing to do it all by yourself, you'll have to.

- When you don't take 100 per cent responsibility for achieving your outcome, you are not working magic, you are playing with luck.

- The only benefit of not taking 100 per cent responsibility for achieving your outcome is that you'll always have someone to blame.

I refocused on my dream and though it took another three years before I finally made the decision to focus on my new company full-time, I got there.

What if you're really prepared to go for it?

"I've come to believe that each of us has a personal calling that's as unique as a fingerprint – and that the best way to succeed is to discover what you love and then find a way to offer it to others in the form of service, working hard, and also allowing the energy of the universe to lead you.**"**

                                                    Oprah Winfrey

Think about people you know who have been very successful at achieving their goals. What has made them stand out from the crowd?

Sharon – rebuilding her body with focus and dedication

There is a myth that it's hard to lose weight over the age of 50. Sharon was 52 when she decided it was time for a new body. She was three stone overweight, in poor health and miserable. She had a very specific goal which was to lose three stone in three months – a tall order for anyone. She was motivated by a vision she had of herself being able to buy a new and younger looking wardrobe, and, most importantly, of her health improving as a result of the weight loss. I couldn't help but notice her focus and determination. Her vision gave her a discipline that drove her forward towards her goal. Quick results led to the motivation to keep at it. Even over Christmas she stuck to her new routine of eating less and exercising more. She experimented with a number of ways to shift the weight without becoming obsessed with any of them. Within three months she had done it, and a year later the weight is still off. She is in much better health, looks younger and is full of vitality. She loves her new body.

Exercise 7

New goal generator

This exercise helps you to visualise your goal. The brain doesn't know the difference between that which is real and that which is imagined and this exercise assists the brain to believe that the goal is achievable. It will even help you to establish new neural pathways in your brain. In fact, if we continuously carry out a new behaviour for 30 days, a new neural pathway is established. I recommend that you do the exercise once a day for a month and you will notice the difference. It only takes 5–10 minutes per day.

1. Close your eyes, stop for a moment and imagine that in front of you is 'another you'.

2. It's the other you that has achieved your goal.

3. Imagine what you'd look like, feel like, sound like, having achieved your goal.

4. If it isn't quite how you'd like it, make the adjustments that make you feel absolutely fantastic. Connect the picture to the feelings and make sure that you feel it in the now and not as you imagine it in the future.

5. When you're satisfied with the other you, step into them, looking through their eyes. Notice how it feels to have achieved your goal. Notice your new perspective, behaviours and beliefs about yourself.

6. Now think of a situation that you would like to view from your new perspective of having achieved your goal. How are things going to be so much better now?

7. For the next few weeks act as if the other you is really you – and notice the difference.

Tip: You get out what you put in so make your goals stretching, specific and get seriously excited about them!

Chapter

4

'Be careful what you wish for.'

Ancient proverb

Focus on what you want

If I were to ask you now not to think about a blue tree, what do you think about in order not to think about it? That's right – a blue tree. Our minds cannot process a negative. I remember, when my kids were small, asking my son not to put his peanut butter sandwich in the video player – oh dear... If you produce a thought or internal representation of something you don't want that's exactly what you'll get. The opposite is, of course, to **focus on what you want**. This is very important when working towards your goals. If you focus on what you don't want to achieve or you focus on all the things that could get in the way of you achieving your goal, then be warned – you are likely to create exactly those things for yourself. How exactly does that happen? We'll be exploring that in this chapter.

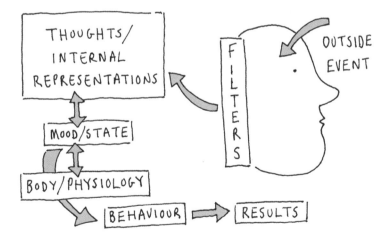

NLP communication model

Have you ever been at the same event as someone else and found out later that they had a completely different experience of it from you? Think back, for example, to the last time you went to a family wedding and then discussed the event with a relative afterwards. How different was their experience from yours? How is it possible that you could both be in the same place at the same time and yet experience the event so differently? Perhaps you even ended up wondering if you had actually been at the same wedding.

NLP communication model

Every second of every day, as we go about our daily lives, external events are impacting on our thoughts. We might be chatting with a friend or enjoying a great meal with our partner, or at work with our colleagues or out with our children. It doesn't matter. Those events enter our nervous system after going through our personal filters. Each of us has a different set of filters, even if we come from the same family. The filters include our values and beliefs about the world, our memories and our experiences. That's why two people can witness the same event yet experience it differently. It's like every external event going through a personal sieve and my sieve has different holes in it from yours. We end up with a different experience and neither of them is the actual event itself. It can never be the actual event because we change reality as it goes through our filters.

Once the information enters our filters, we make pictures in our heads, hear sounds, have feelings and we talk to ourselves. We refer to these images in NLP as 'internal representations'. They are just that – representations of reality; **not** reality itself. Your own internal representations are unique to you. They are your way of perceiving the world – if you like, your map of the world or your thoughts. If we create a positive internal representation supported by positive self-talk about an event, we will be in a more positive emotional state, which in turn means we are more likely to get the result we want. An emotional state is the sum total of all the neurological processes occurring inside you at any one time. A simpler way of thinking about it is that an emotional state is the mood you are in at any given moment.

We've all experienced unhelpful moods such as anger, fear and sadness. In contrast, we've also experienced positive moods such as motivation, determination and happiness. This is very important because all behaviour and therefore our results are mood dependent. For example, if we are feeling motivated and powerful as we go into an interview situation, our results are likely to be much more positive than if we are feeling nervous and anxious. Anything amazing that you have done will be as a result of the mood you were in at the time.

The really clever thing is that we can programme our minds to be in positive moods whenever we need them to be. We can choose the way we represent the world to ourselves. This opens up fantastic opportunities, and I'm going to show you how to do it.

Exercise 8

Taking control of your mood

First of all, imagine that it's Saturday night and you have bought your lottery ticket for the weekend. You have chosen the same numbers as you have done since the lottery started. You then pick up your favourite takeaway and you go back home. You've bought enough for two as you've invited your neighbour in for the evening. You are great friends. You are sitting comfortably on your couch drinking a delicious glass of wine and relaxing while you wait for your neighbour to arrive.

I'd like you to put yourself in that situation now. Imagine floating down inside your body as you sit in front of the TV feeling relaxed. How would you feel? What would you be wearing? What would you be saying to yourself? The lottery programme comes on and you watch the draw as usual. You feel anticipation tingling inside as the time of the draw gets nearer. You watch closely as the first ball drops down through the machine. It's your number. You suddenly sit up straight and start to take more interest in the programme. The second ball comes down and it's also your number. You can feel your heart beginning to beat more rapidly now. You become fixated on the TV. The third and fourth balls come down and they are also your numbers. What would you feel like right now? I mean really feel like? Can you feel the excitement rising in your body? If not, why not? Make it happen. The fifth ball drops and you can hardly bear to watch. Yes, it's also your number – one more to go. You are already thinking about how you will spend the money when the last ball drops down. It seems to take for ever to fall out of the chute – and through your fingers which are covering your eyes at this moment as if you're watching a horror movie you see the number. Yes! It's your number. You are a lottery winner.

Stand up. Look up to the ceiling and put the biggest smile on your face that you have ever experienced and say 'yes, yes, yes' continually to yourself in your head – maybe it's not the best time to do this if you're on the tube or train, though of course it might get you a seat! Then as you continue to look up at the ceiling, try your hardest to feel miserable. Come on – really try. It's impossible, isn't it?

Then you begin to look around for your ticket. You look everywhere in the house. You thought you put it in the normal place but it's not there. You turn out all the drawers in your whole house. As you move from room to room your actions become more frantic. Still the ticket is nowhere to be found. The ticket is lost along with the £2 million lottery prize. How would you be feeling now? Really put yourself into that experience. Slump your shoulders, sink your head. Put a big frown on your face. Now try your hardest to feel happy. Come on – really try. It's impossible, isn't it?

There's a knock at the door and you answer it. Your neighbour is standing there. You'd forgotten about her in all the excitement and then panic. She asks you what on earth is the matter. Before you can tell her, she's handed you the lottery ticket that she's just found on your front step. Fortunately, she hadn't been watching the lottery programme or else you may never have seen her again! So now you have the winning ticket in your hand. How would you be feeling right now? Float down inside your lottery winning body and imagine how you would look and feel. What would you be saying to yourself? As before, stand up, look up to the ceiling and put the biggest smile on your face that you have ever experienced and say 'yes, yes, yes' continually to yourself in your head. Well done. You can sit down again now!

The purpose of that exercise is to give you a personal experience of the link between your thoughts, mood, body and ultimately the result that you produce. It's actually impossible to think of an unpleasant situation when you have a big grin on your face, and vice versa. Changes in our posture, breathing, muscle tension and facial expressions will affect the way we feel in an instant. If your body is tense it will even produce different chemicals from the ones it releases when it is relaxed. If you experiment in using your body in a different way you will experience life differently. Next time you feel less than confident and you need to be confident, put yourself in a confident posture, act as if, and notice the difference. The most important thing for you to know is that it's impossible to feel bad and at the same time be having good thoughts. That's because your thoughts and your physiology cause feelings as we have seen. If you are feeling bad, it's because you are thinking thoughts that are making you feel bad. This will affect the result that you create for yourself.

In *Silent Messages*, Albert Mehrabian wrote that understanding the difference between words and meaning is a vital capability for effective communications and relationships. His model is particularly useful in illustrating the importance of factors other than words alone when trying to convey meaning (as the speaker) or interpret meaning (as the listener). He discovered that people tend to believe the facial expression that they see more than the actual words spoken. He found that when people are talking about their feelings or attitudes, voice tonality and facial expression account for 93 per cent of the meaning inferred by the people in his study – voice tonality for 38 per cent and facial expression for 55 per cent. Words accounted for just 7 per cent. So, if I tell you that I'm really excited about something but I'm talking in a slow monotone voice, and if I'm slumped in a chair looking bored as I talk, you are likely to put far more faith in my facial expressions than in the words that I use.

This is important because not only is there a link between our thoughts, mood, body and result – as we experienced in the lottery experiment – in terms of how we feel inside, but other people will also notice and interpret the meaning of how we project ourselves to the outside world.

Exercise 9

The power of the mind

Let's experience this for ourselves. Imagine that you are meeting your boss to discuss your annual appraisal. This job is really important to you as you have some debts to pay off and it's the first time you've had the chance of a successful long-term career. First of all, I want you to focus on being really anxious and concerned that you will get a negative appraisal and that this may sabotage your long-term success in the role. You've been worried about this meeting and you haven't been able to sleep very well because of it. You feel under pressure to get a good result from the session because so much depends on it.

Now hold that internal representation in your head with the associated pictures, feelings, sounds and thoughts.

As you step through your boss's office door, write down the impact this will have on:

- your thoughts

- your mood

- your body posture

- your behaviour

- your results.

Clear the screen. This time I want you to focus on being really confident about your results and successes so far in the new job. This meeting is a small step between where you are now and getting to the next level. You are totally convinced the meeting will go well and you will get what you want.

Now hold that internal representation in your head with the associated pictures, feelings, sounds and thoughts.

Write down the impact this will have on:

- your thoughts

- your mood

- your body posture

- your behaviour

- your results.

What did you notice in that exercise? Which internal representation is more likely to get you what you want? The positive
one, of course. Yet, how often do we sabotage ourselves by
thinking negative thoughts before the event has even happened?
We know already that as our body language accounts for 55 per
cent of the impact of a face to face communication, we don't
even have to say anything for our boss to know how we really
feel. In the first example, we may say the right words but our
body language will give away our true feelings, and the boss
will pick up on the incongruency between the two. They will be
far less likely to cooperate with us than in the second example,
when we appear confident and focused on our result and there
is congruency between what we say and what we do. Think
about it for a moment. I bet your best results have always been
achieved when you've been in a positive state of mind.

Michael – aligning thoughts and deeds

Michael played tennis regularly. However, he was enjoying it
less and less. He loved to play doubles tennis tournaments
but lately had lost most of his matches in the first round, and
fewer and fewer people wanted to partner with him. He was
close to giving up this hobby until he heard about the power of
our thoughts. For the first time he paid attention to his thoughts
and discovered that he had been unconsciously focused on all
the things that could go wrong in his matches. No surprise then
that he ended up attracting those things to himself. Once he
was consciously aware of this, he began to change his thoughts
to positive ones and now has a queue of people wanting to play
doubles with him again.

The link between goals and the communication model

"Thoughts create things." Mike Dooley

How we respond to the information coming into our nervous system and the internal representations that we create is

therefore very significant. Experts have estimated that our nervous systems, through our five senses, are bombarded by two million bits of data each second of the day. We can only digest 126 bits of that data, which boils down to seven (plus or minus two) manageable chunks each second. Our filters take out the rest of the data by deleting, distorting and generalising information. That's a lot of data to get rid of. No wonder that two people remember the same event differently, as the 126 bits of data that you focus on will be different to the 126 bits of data that I focus on. What we delete, distort and generalise depends upon the values and beliefs we have and our memories and experiences. For example, if I believe that marriage is a commendable institution and my friend believes it is a waste of time, we are likely to have a very different experience of our other friend's wedding as we each filter the event through our different belief systems. Are you with me on this as it's very important?

One of the key assumptions in NLP is that 'the map is not the territory'. In this model the map (our internal representation) is not the territory that it represents. Our every experience is something that we literally make up inside our heads. We **do not experience reality directly,** since we are always deleting, distorting and generalising the information as it comes into our nervous system. Essentially, there is only what we create **inside** of us and then project to the outside world. We can never experience the purity of the territory without it being filtered first.

What is this thing called RAS?

I think of our conscious mind as our **goal setter** and our unconscious mind as our **goal getter.** The conscious mind is the goal setter because the goal setting process is a very logical, conscious process. The unconscious mind is called the **goal getter** because of the part of your brain known as the *reticular activating system* – or RAS for short. Your RAS plays a vital part in your ability to achieve goals via your unconscious mind. As I mentioned in Chapter 3, I don't believe that it's necessary to work out detailed plans to achieve your goal. The important thing is to set your attention in the right direction. All you need to do then is leave the delivery to your unconscious mind. You'll be astonished at how quickly you begin to attract to yourself things and people who will help you to achieve your goal.

Recently I was in a busy airport terminal when I discovered that my flight was delayed by two hours. I was feeling pretty annoyed and frustrated about the delay so I decided to spend the time spoiling myself by eating and drinking something nice. I went to the smart fish bar and ordered a prawn salad and a glass of chilled white wine. There was a lot of noise going on around me – hundreds of people talking, music playing, announcements being made and luggage carriers bouncing over the ground. I paid very little attention to any of it though as I sat on my bar stool enjoying my meal. True, I heard a general background noise, but I didn't bother to listen to each individual sound. Then suddenly, an announcement for the last call for my flight came over the PA system. The delay had been resolved and in fact the flight was only 30 minutes late after all. I heard the last call for my flight followed by my name and a message saying that my baggage was about to be removed from the flight. Suddenly, my attention was full on and I gulped down the last of my wine and ran to the departure gate as fast as I could. My RAS was the automatic mechanism inside my brain that brought the relevant information to my attention and saved me from missing an important flight.

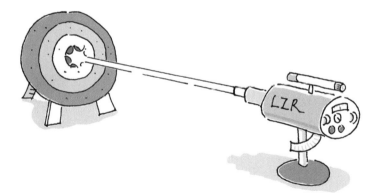

Your reticular activating system acts as a gateway between your conscious mind and your unconscious mind. It takes instructions from your conscious mind and passes them on to your unconscious. For example, the instruction might be to 'listen out for anyone saying my name'. This is why you should be careful what you wish for. Your unconscious mind will be looking out for it even if your conscious mind is elsewhere.

Triggering your RAS

There are features of your RAS that make it an essential tool for achieving your goals. When you set your goal you create a very specific internal representation of it with pictures, sounds, feelings, tastes and smells in your conscious mind. The RAS will then pass this on to your unconscious – which will then help you to achieve the goal. It does this by bringing to your attention all the relevant information which otherwise might have remained as 'background noise'. Or, in other words, your RAS ensures that the 126 bits of information that you focus on is information that will support your goal. Focusing on two or three key areas or a single goal does something special to your behaviour. It triggers your RAS. We know our brains are bombarded by thousands of messages each second. Everything you see, hear, smell, feel and touch is a message entering your brain. The RAS filters through *all* these messages and decides which ones get page one treatment – that is, arouse the brain.

Paying attention

One of the things I've noticed from modelling entrepreneurs is that they pay attention to the things which are important to them at the time. If their dominant thoughts are about creating a new business, they'll start seeing other businesses and ideas. They hear conversations about new business ventures. They'll pick up ideas relating to new business ventures and even see things around them in a different way and relate it back to business.

In other words, your RAS will reject or ignore anything unrelated to your focus and highlight anything that is even remotely related to the important issue – in this instance, the new business venture. When we have goals, our RAS directs us to possibilities that support us in achieving our goals that we didn't notice before. Have you ever been in a situation where you made a decision about something and suddenly you began to make useful connections to people and things that could support you? At the time you may have thought of that as a coincidence, but what if it was your RAS taking instructions from your conscious mind to seek out what you needed? For example, when you are considering buying a certain model of car, have you noticed how you begin to see that model everywhere? You might have justifiably wondered if they were there before or not. Or if you have kids, do you remember when you or your partner first got pregnant and you began to see babies and prams everywhere? Where did they all suddenly appear from?

Be careful what you focus on

In contrast, if you focus on what you don't want your RAS will do an excellent job of delivering that to you. Have you ever tried saying to a child 'Don't touch'? The child's brain cannot process a negative and so they focus on the word 'touch' and they go ahead and touch. If you want to lose weight and you focus on 'not being fat', guess what? Your RAS will focus on being fat and doing a really good job for you. If you focus on 'not being in debt', your RAS will focus on debt and attract it to you. If you're looking at a mountain of debt and feeling terrible about it, that's the signal you're putting into the universe. If you focus on what you don't want, your RAS is really obedient. When you think of what you don't want and you focus on it intently, then your RAS will give you exactly what you want, every time. When you focus on something no matter what it happens to be, you are really calling it into existence. Are you following this? So it becomes a **self-fulfilling prophecy**. You have a choice right now. Do you want to believe that things just happen and it's the luck of the draw what happens to you? Or do you want to believe and know that your life experience is in your own hands and that good can come into your life because of the way you think and what you focus on? No one would ever deliberately attract what they don't want into their lives. It simply comes from a lack of awareness. For you, this has changed for ever because you cannot unlearn what you now know.

If you don't believe me, run this experiment with a child. Tell them what they should do **instead of** what they shouldn't do and notice the difference in their behaviour. Parents and teachers are all missing a huge trick if they don't do this! A friend of mine asked me to go along to his presentation skills training to review his programme and to give him feedback. I counted on the first day that he told his students over 80 times what not to do: 'Don't move'…'Don't wave your arms about'…'Don't panic if you forget what to say.' The next day after we talked about my feedback the students did so much better, and the difference was that they were told what they should do instead: 'Stand still'... 'Keep your arms at your side'... 'Keep calm if you forget what to do next.'

If you have no goals in life, then your RAS has nothing to go for. If you are drifting from one thing to the next with no focus, then your RAS does not have any clear instructions what to seek out for you. I'm sure we all know people who lead chaotic lives, not settling for anything for very long. Maybe you have experienced life like that up until this moment. Now there are no more excuses. Get your RAS working for you, as it does it very well – use all 126 bits of information entering your nervous system every second of your life to focus on what you want.

I talked in Chapter 3 of letting go of the specifics of how you achieve your goal – because otherwise you will limit the opportunities your RAS can present to you. Let's also revisit why it's important to let go of it not being OK for you to not get your goal. As I mentioned in Chapter 3, this may sound contradictory to what I said earlier in the book about your goal being compelling. However, as I noted, if it's not OK for you not to get your goal you will focus on your anxieties about not getting the goal. If you focus on and place your attention on what you don't want, you are likely to attract exactly that thing to you. We can understand now how that can happen because your RAS will only present to you the evidence to confirm that you were right all along and that will be the end of that!

Matthew – focusing on dangerous things

I had a client recently who came to see me after he had lost a successful business. The business had gone bankrupt after initially being very profitable. As he was telling me the story of what had happened I noticed in his language how he started to worry about losing the company after it had taken off so quickly and so well. It was almost as if it was too good to be true for him and he became obsessed with losing it all. It didn't take long before he stopped noticing the successes of his company and focused only on those things that didn't go to plan. He lost the business.

Deletions, distortions and generalisations

I spoke earlier of our primary filters, which are to distort, delete and generalise information coming into our nervous system. So what specifically happens when we delete, distort and generalise data?

Deletions

Let's have some fun for a moment. Read to yourself the text you see in the triangle below.

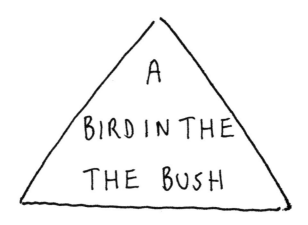

More than likely you said to yourself 'a bird in the bush'. If this is what you said, then you didn't notice that the word 'the' is repeated twice. Look again! Your brain does not expect to see the second 'the' there and so it deletes it.

Second test. Count every 'f' in the text below:

FINISHED FILES ARE THE RE

SULT OF YEARS OF SCIENTI

FIC STUDY COMBINED WITH

THE EXPERIENCE OF YEARS...

Anyone who counts all six 'f's first time around is a genius. Three is normal, four is quite rare. In this example, our brains do not process the word 'of' – it gets deleted.

If I were to ask you right now to think about how it feels to sit on your chair, you will immediately become aware of the feeling of your backside on the chair and your back against the back of the chair, although previously you had deleted the information as 'useless'.

Our ability to delete portions of the barrage of input is essential to our survival. The interesting question is, what are you currently deleting that you need to pay attention to in order to achieve your goals? What are the possibilities that you haven't noticed yet that will make the difference between success and never getting there?

Generalisations

We use generalisations to speed up our learning process. One of the great things about NLP is that it resists generalisations and encourages us to take each context on its own merits. However, for most people beliefs drive all their actions, and beliefs are shaped by generalisations. These beliefs then become limitations for future decisions about who you are and what you are capable of. For example, if you have experienced a disappointing relationship, you might now believe that all future relationships will be the same. Your emotional state and physiology will reflect this, as will your behaviour and results – you are not likely to attract the right kind of person or make a relationship work under these conditions. Perhaps you now believe that you're not good enough to achieve your goals because your parents and teachers have told you that in the past. Because of your generalisation, your RAS only notices the times when you didn't get what you wanted. It misses the examples of when you have been very successful. What generalisations do you have about yourself that will impact on your goals until you deal with them? Do you use phrases like 'I never...' or 'I always...'? We will work on these in Chapter 5.

Distortions

We attach meanings to things that are our 'mind-reads'. The trouble is that we then confuse them with reality. For example, my bank manager looked at me in a disinterested way when I asked him for a loan. I could take that to mean that he will refuse my request. However, it may be that he just wants to leave work early – nothing to do with my request! Sometimes we arbitrarily interpret reality and we end up distorting its meaning. We attach meanings that don't exist and end up making huge assumptions. A glance or a gesture may have thousands of meanings and it is so easy to interpret the wrong one. Distortions can get in the way of our goals when we attach the wrong meaning to important issues. Find out a more accurate meaning by asking! The people who are most successful check things out; they say things as they are and they are not afraid to give and ask for feedback in order to get more accurate information.

The unconscious mind

At this point it's probably time to say something about the unconscious mind and why it's important in NLP. The 'unconscious' refers to that part of mental functioning of which we are often unaware. Our unconscious by definition includes most of what is simply not conscious. This includes what is actively repressed from conscious thought, such as negative emotions and painful experiences, as well as all our memories and our true feelings about things. It is believed that our unconscious mind holds all our memories of everything that we have ever experienced. We cannot hold that data consciously or else we would be overloaded with information very quickly. Our unconscious mind often presents issues to us for resolution. Remember the last time something important popped into your head. That is your unconscious mind making you aware of things. For example, if you make a conscious decision about something that you then get a negative feeling about, that is your unconscious making you aware of a potential issue. Often thoughts come into our minds during the day and through dreams of things that we need to pay attention to – they come from an unconscious level. If we ignore these warnings the unconscious mind will often present in a more serious way, sometimes even through illness. NLP teaches us to pay attention to our unconscious mind and to trust the signals it gives to us. I recommend developing your intuitive perception or unconscious knowing. When you learn to trust your unconscious mind, you will begin to recognise messages that come from your body in response to new people, situations, places and ideas. Your unconscious mind never lies. Hidden, like the man behind the curtain in *The Wizard of Oz*, the unconscious mind directs your thoughts, feelings and health.

The link between mind and body

Over the past 30 years, scientists have discovered an undeniable link between the mind and the body. The vehicle that the mind and body use to communicate with each other is the chemistry of emotion. The chemicals in question are molecules, short chains of amino acids called peptides and receptors, that are believed to be the 'biochemical correlate of emotion'. The peptides can be found in your brain, but also in your stomach, your muscles, your glands and all your major organs, sending messages back and forth.

Our cells are eavesdropping on our thoughts every second of our lives. So our emotions have a deciding influence on our health as the neuropeptides and their receptors are in constant communication with the immune system. Viruses use the same receptors to enter the cells, as do the neuropeptides we release when we are experiencing elevated moods. Is this the reason why depressed people have a tendency to get sick more often whilst those who are happy and relaxed stay healthy? Is that why if we are feeling sick and have taken to our bed, and then the person we've fancied for months calls and asks us out, within minutes we are in a different emotional state and ready to go out? It's because the neuropeptides flood out the virus molecules and release energy that help us to feel much better. It seems to be that our health reflects the emotions we are feeling and the emotions follow the thoughts we think. Something to think about...

Making sense of all this

Let me pull all of these strands together. In this chapter we have explored the link between our thoughts, our emotional state, our physiology, our behaviour and ultimately our results. We can never experience the outside world in its purest sense as we always perceive external events through our personal filters. Everyone has different filters so we experience events in different ways.

Because our nervous system cannot process negatives, it's very important to focus on what you want as opposed to what you don't want. If you focus on the wrong thing, then you will get the wrong thing.

Our brains have the capacity to process huge amounts of information every second of our lives. We need to have goals to give our unconscious minds and our RAS something to work on. The purpose of your RAS is vital in the goal-getting process as it will search out the people, information and events that will most serve you. Goals give your RAS something to focus on. If you have no goals, you will drift through life and your results will be adversely affected.

The quality of your thoughts will also have an impact on the well-being of your whole being, not just your mind. As your cells eavesdrop on all your thoughts, it's vital that your thoughts, and your emotions are supportive to your system. Human cells have evolved to a formidable state of intelligence. Imagine if you spent your life focusing on negative thoughts or feelings – what damaging suggestions will you be giving to the rest of your body?

Tip: Nothing has any power over you other than that which you give it through your daily thoughts.

Chapter

5

'Why be yourself when you can be someone so much better?'

Richard Bandler

Who am I?

The Greeks inscribed the words 'Know thyself' at the Temple of Apollo in Athens. In more recent times, the same words were inscribed in Latin above the door of the Oracle's house in the film *The Matrix*. Why is self-knowledge so important, as we define our goals and start to focus on what we want? If our goals are fully aligned with who we really are and what is most important to us, then achieving them will be much easier – because only then will we be motivated to do whatever it takes to move ahead. It's as simple as that. Also, if we know our own strengths and development areas we can make some choices about the best way to achieve our goals. For example, if I learn that I operate best when I have variety in what I do and when I'm working with others, I'm not going to get my best results working in a similar routine each day entirely on my own. So the bottom line is that knowing yourself is *key* to personal leadership and strong personal leadership achieves goals.

In this chapter we're going to learn more about our personalities through three different NLP-based lenses. In the last chapter we learned about our filters which we unconsciously use to manage the data coming into our nervous system. We use our filters to delete, distort and generalise this data to make it manageable for ourselves. In this chapter we're going to explore three of these filters in more detail as they are critical to how we view the world. Shelle Rose Charvet describes our filters as:

"like a door through which we interact with the world... (our filters) simply describe the form of our door, what specifically we let in and out in a given situation.**"**

Firstly we're going to explore the key 'meta programmes' that give us an insight into how we are programmed to behave in certain situations. If we can begin to understand and predict how we are likely to behave, we can also start to adapt or change our behaviour to become more effective. Secondly, we're going to learn about our preferred style of communicating with the outside world and, finally, we'll learn how to access our 'unconscious' values in many different situations. Learning about all three will have the effect of bringing much information about who we are and how we behave to a conscious level of your awareness – maybe for the first time ever. Are you ready for an exciting journey of self-discovery? Let's begin with meta programmes.

Meta programmes

A simple way of thinking about meta programmes is to think of them as your patterns of behaviour or – even more more simply – as your personality. They are largely unconscious in so far as you normally react without consciously thinking about it. *They are deep-rooted mental programmes which automatically filter our experiences and guide and direct your thought processes.* Different combinations of meta programmes lead to significant differences in behaviour from one person to the next. Learning about your meta programmes will help you decide which elements of your personality are helpful in your personal development journey and which you'd like to change in some way. Maybe you've had feedback in the past about your behaviour and have not known what to do about that. The first step to changing your behaviour is to be aware of how you react. Then you can start to make different choices about what to do in future.

Leslie Cameron-Bandler (ex-wife of Richard Bandler) originally came up with 60 patterns. Roger Bailey, a student of Leslie's, reduced the number of patterns from 60 to 14. We are going to explore eight which are particularly helpful for discovering the basics of your personality. Before we start, here are some things to bear in mind about meta programmes:

- Those people in your life that you get on with best are probably people with a similar profile to you. Equally, people you get on with least well are likely to have a very different profile to you.

- No one style or profile is better than another. They are just different models of the world.

- Your meta programmes may change over time as you learn new information or experience significant events in your life.

- You can begin to identify another person's meta programmes from the language they use and/or their behaviours.

- Caution, generalisation ahead: meta programmes are generalisations of behaviour. We are all different. Yet, we have preferences in our behaviour that help us predict how we and others will behave in certain situations.

Exercise 10

Holding up the mirror

Answer these questions as quickly as you can. Don't even try to over-analyse. Go with what you are most like in each situation.

1. When you get involved in a new situation do you:
   a. Usually act quickly?
   b. Make a complete study of all the consequences then act?

2. How do you know when you've done something well? Do you:
   a. Know within yourself?
   b. Have to ask others for feedback?

3. In your life do you:
   a. Prefer to stick with what is tried and tested?
   b. Prefer to have variety and change?

4. In day-to-day conversations with other people do you:
   a. Ask lots of questions to get down to all the details?
   b. Prefer a quick overview of what's been going on?

5. When you are in a social situation do you:

   a. Love to people watch and notice everything around you?

   b. Prefer to keep your head down or chat to a friend, ignoring everyone else?

6. Did you choose your current job because:

   a. It gives you lots of different options and possibilities?

   b. You felt you had no choice?

7. If someone you knew quite well said to you 'I'm cold' would you:

   a. Feel compelled to jump up and close the windows or get them a jumper?

   b. Find the comment interesting but do nothing about it?

8. If you didn't like what one of your friends was doing would you:

   a. Come straight to the point?

   b. Give lots of hints and clues to avoid telling them how you truly felt?

Turn to Appendix 1 for the answers and descriptions of each behavioural style. Circle your choices below:

My meta programmes

Q1 (a) Proactive (b) Reactive

Q2 (a) Internal (b) External

Q3 (a) Sameness (b) Difference

Q4 (a) Specific (b) Global

Q5 (a) Attention on others (b) Attention on self

Q6 (a) Options (b) Procedures

Q7 (a) Inferential (b) Literal (listener)

Q8 (a) Literal (b) Inferential (speaker)

Changing your personality

Did you get any surprises? Are there any elements you'd like to change? For example, if you are a reactive, sameness, procedures person you may find that you have been your own worst enemy up until now. You are likely to have been struggling to move outside of the Grey Zone because it means moving into the unknown, which has probably been too scary for you. If you are this person, then take small steps and do not run before you can walk as that will be too much for you. For example, to become more proactive, start to take action quicker than normal. Stop waiting for others to tell you what to do. Come up with some relatively 'risk-free' ideas of your own and experiment. I guarantee that you'll surprise yourself. If you are sameness and you want to become more flexible, start to break out of your normal routine. Go to a new restaurant for a change, buy a new style of clothing or a new colour you don't normally wear, go someplace new for your holiday. You see, you can take small steps towards enjoying change. If you want to move from procedures to options, then ask yourself what would you really like to do for yourself? Something you 'want to do' and not something you 'have to' do. Again, take small steps – start with a new hobby or take some time for 'you' to relax in whatever way you enjoy. Build up to those bigger goals!

If you discover that you are very 'external' and you find it hard to do anything without someone else's approval, again start to take small steps and pay more attention to your own 'internal' intuition. Ask yourself if you've actually been criticised in the past for something? The chances are you won't have been. What is it that you're really afraid of? Often externals are limited by their own personal belief system – we are going to tackle this in Chapter 7. If you've found that you are both an inferential listener and speaker, you may have found it tough to get others to take action around you. Instead, you're the one wasting energy on tasks that may not even need to be done. Experiment with more direct feedback in areas that don't matter too much and gradually build to those areas that do. Check yourself next time you are about to jump up when someone says 'I'm cold'. If you find you are a literal listener and speaker, it may be the reason why others are sometimes offended by your way of behaving. There are ways of softening what you have to say without losing the impact. If you're global and have been having challenges communicating with another person, it may be because they are specific – or vice versa. For example, I notice this in couples counselling. One member says to the other, 'how was your day?' The other says 'it was fine'. The first person then begins a 10-minute rendition of everything they have done that day including the price of bread. The other person has long drifted off and been thinking of other things! If you don't get the response you want from another, maybe you need to become more global or more specific to build a stronger rapport with them. Finally, if you have attention on self, ask yourself how will this affect your ability to get on with others? Will they experience you as disinterested or even self-ish? Take some time to practise, noticing more by bringing your attention to the outside – you'll see the world in a different light.

Susie – going for gold

Susie's profile was differences, with procedures and inferential in her speaking style. She had joined the family business straight from school as it was expected of her and her family needed her. The business was a successful catering company which had slowly grown to a team of 50 staff. They supplied some of the big-gest restaurant chains in the country. Susie joined the finance team and over the years was promoted to become the finance director of the business. She was now in her early forties and very unhappy. She was really bored with the routine of her job and yet felt a strong requirement to 'toe the family line' and do what was expected of her. She was also very reticent to telling her parents how she really felt. Over the years, she had hinted about her true desire to train to become an architect, which was a much better fit with her creative flair, but something had always held her back. She came to me for a breakthrough session because she had become very depressed about her situation. She was in the Awful Zone and something had to shift. Once she understood more about her personality, we began to work on new strategies for the future. She became more options-driven and focused on what she wanted for herself for the first time ever. She also adopted a more direct speaking style and told her parents how unhappy she was. They were disappointed yet wanted her to be happy and gave their blessing for her to do something different. She is now studying for an architectural degree.

Communication styles

In NLP these are referred to *representational systems* – for simplicity I'm going to refer to them as our communications styles. It all started when Bandler and Grinder noticed that people spoke using three different styles of language – visual, auditory or kinaesthetic. A fourth category 'audio digital' was added later. They already knew, of course, that people structure their experience of the world through the five senses – seeing, hearing, feeling, tasting and smelling. They began to realise that there was a link to a matching set of 'internal senses' which they later called 'representational systems'. In other words, what we actually perceive are representations or models of what each of our sensory organs transmits to us. Another way of describing these would be preferences in our thinking patterns. If I say to you the word 'sea' what comes to mind? Did you see a picture of the sea, or hear the sound of the waves or remember the feeling of hot sand under your toes? Or recall some interesting statistics about the sea? Your answer will give you a clue as to your preferred style. Although we all use all of these four styles of communicating, we have a preference towards one.

Exercise 11

Which is your preferred communication style?

Now let's find out for sure. For each of the following statements, please mark which answer is most like you using the following system to indicate your preferences:

Closest to describing you (allocate 4 points)

Next best description (allocate 3 points)

Next best (allocate 2 points)

Least descriptive of you (allocate 1 point).

Then add up your total scores for A, then B, then C, then D.

1. I prefer to chill out by:

   3 A — having a massage.

   4 B — listening to music.

---

1 C — looking at beautiful scenery.

2 D — learning more information about a subject that interests me.

2. If I agree with you, I'm most likely to say:

2 A — that feels right.

4 B — I hear what you say.

1 C — I see what you mean.

3 D — that makes sense.

3. When buying something new, I'm most likely to:

2 A — go for what feels most comfortable.

4 B — react to what is said to me and/or the sounds (if relevant) of the item.

1 C — choose what looks best.

3 D — set a strict criteria for what I want.

4. When choosing a restaurant I go for a place:

1 A — that has a great ambiance and comfortable furniture.

4 B — that has my kind of music.

2 C — that has great décor and fab views.

3 D — that has been reviewed and recommended by various critics.

5. I get on best with people who:

4 A — are very touchy feely.

1 B — I can really tune in to.

2 C — get to the point and make decisions quickly.

3 D — give me lots of relevant information.

Questionnaire answers

Make a note below of your total scores for A, B, C or D.

A's (kinaesthetic/feelings) —

B's (auditory) —

C's (visual) —

D's (audio digital / logical) —

Your highest score indicates the style that you use most to experience the world. If your highest score was kinaesthetic, you process information from the outside world through your feelings and are unlikely to take action until something feels 'right' to you. You act on your 'gut feel' or intuition a lot. If you are auditory, something needs to 'sound right' for you to take action. If you are visual, you process using pictures and you will only act if something 'looks right' to you. Finally, if you are audio digital or logical, you will only act if something makes sense to you, and often after a thorough review of all the facts.

What's really fascinating is that each of these styles also has characteristics that are common to that style and uses language that represents that preferred communicating style. This means not only can you recognise your own style but you can also start to spot someone else's style easily. And, at the same time, remember that this is a model based on generalisations of behaviour. We are all different and we do not *only* operate from one style and nor do other people. What follows are generalisations of each style which you may or may not recognise in yourself and others. In my own personal experience of working with individuals and groups I find them regularly to be true.

Characteristics of the different styles

Kinaesthetic

Kinaesthetic people take their time to process information because they literally process through their feelings and it can take some moments to get in touch with them. They breathe from the bottom of their lungs and tend to speak and move around in a deliberate way. They may be physically larger than the other styles as they are more alert to bodily needs and comforts including hunger and eating so their frames tend to fill out. They have a slower and lower pitched voice which comes from breathing into the lower portion of their lungs. They respond to touch and physical reward and love to get stuck into things to learn. They stand up close to others to feel connected. They wear comfortable clothes and live in a comfortable environment.

Auditory

Auditory people tend to be slim and often seen with their arms folded and their head tilted to one side as they concentrate on listening to what is being said. They breathe from the middle of their chest. They often talk to themselves and are very distracted by noise. For example, on one of my seven-day NLP Practitioner trainings, one of my auditory students gave me feedback on the last day that the course had changed her life but could I wear quieter shoes next time! They remember things verbally and can repeat back exactly what you said to them. They often remember things that were said to them months if not years before. As you might expect, they enjoy talking on the phone and listening to music. They are particularly sensitive to tone of voice and they memorise things by steps, procedures and sequences.

Visual

Visual people tend to process information quicker than the other styles because they process through pictures in their heads and they can change these pictures very fast. This happens unconsciously. They can get frustrated with the slower pace taken by others. They are tend to thinner than the other styles, maybe because they tend to move around faster. They like to stand tall and often stand back from the crowd so they can see what is going on clearly. They like to keep more personal space than other styles and will move backwards if you get too close. They will want the seat in the restaurant that gives them the best vantage point to watch what is going on. They are often well dressed and like to 'stand out' in the crowd and they enjoy the people/places/things around them to look good too. They are not good at remembering verbal instructions, preferring to memorise using pictures. They tend to breathe from the tops of their lungs and speak faster than the other styles because their voices and breathing have to keep up with their thoughts. Finally, they can be disconnected from bodily experiences because the visual portions of their environment command more of their attention, e.g. physical demands such as hunger can go unnoticed.

Audio digital

Audio digitals are flexible and can take on the characteristics of the other systems. Not one of the styles identified by Bandler and Grinder, this additional style was added later. (It can be found in *Magic of NLP Demystified* by Lewis and Pucelik). You will often notice these people with their arms crossed and one hand resting under their chin in a 'professor'-like pose. They can be disassociated from their feelings as they live their lives in their heads. They may experience tension in the neck and shoulders because of this. They are very logical and practical people who ask lots of questions to make sense of the world around them. They will often ask you for evidence rather than take things on face value.

Remember we all have the ability to behave like any one of these categories at different times, so always trust your experience.

Using your communication style to best advantage

It's important to know your own style. Maybe you had some lightbulb moments for you as you read through those descriptions.

Kinaesthetics are much better at savouring every moment and enjoying each step of the journey. They live life to the full every step of the way. They have great gut instinct and make good choices about what steps to take. They can take longer though to take action and move forwards. They often get stuck in their emotions which prevents them from moving ahead. They do not always have a clear end vision and so it can take them longer to get going on their journey. Everything has to 'feel' right before they can take action and this can delay them.

Lewis and Pucelik said that in Western cultures the proportion of habitual 'auditories' is small in relation to the other categories. This makes it more difficult to make accurate generalisations about them. They may need help developing a clear vision for the future but once they have it they get on with what they need to do. Easily distracted by noise, where they spend their time is important to them. Somewhere quiet which enables them to forge ahead with their ideas is best for them. They are influenced by voice tonality and so need to bear in mind that they might be over-influenced by this in some conversations. For example, if they detect that someone close to them is not keen for them to pursue their goals, they may pay too much attention to that.

If you're visual like me, you have to be aware that your focus can become all consuming and that often you need to be reminded to eat! Almost in contradiction, visuals can also have too much noise going on in their heads at the same time. This can make it difficult to focus and pay attention to priorities. The important thing for visuals to remember with their goals is to focus on one thing at a time and to ensure that they pay attention to their own needs when their goals become all encompassing. Visuals are often great at creating the 'big picture' around their goals. They can see where they want to get to easily. They stand back and set a strategy for the future and then rush ahead at 100 miles an hour taking action. However, sometimes the detail can get lost and they may need someone around them who is good at making sure that they don't miss anything important. They also need to slow down to enjoy the journey at times!

Audio digitals, like kinaesthetics, can get stuck but for very different reasons. Often they spend too much time researching a new idea and building evidence so that they don't take any action towards achieving it. They may spend months or even years comparing the benefits and risks of two different kinds of businesses without ever taking a decision. The risk for them is that they stay in the Grey Zone and are left only with their regrets. However, when they do take action, their approach will be much less risky than that of the other styles. It will be very methodical and they will have dotted every 'i' and crossed every 't' to ensure their goal has the very best chance of success. They tend to be less emotional about each step than the other styles and this can potentially be a risk to them if they are not compelled enough about their goal.

Also pay attention to your lowest score as this area may need some attention and development. For example, if your lowest score is audio digital how can you ensure that you do enough research about your goals to mitigate any potential risk? Maybe there's more evidence you can gather before you start on your journey?

Exercise 12

Communicating with your goals

Consider what you've learned about your communication preferences. Ask yourself two questions:

a. How does your preferred style, ie the one with the highest score, help you in creating your goals?

b. What steps do you need to take to mitigate against your lowest preference causing you any problems?

Lindsey – speeding through life

As I mentioned earlier, I have a very strong visual preference. I was running an NLP Practitioner programme shortly before Christmas. One lunchtime, I suddenly had an idea to buy all my students a Christmas chocolate to put on their seats before their return from the break. I rushed into a well-known shop and chose a brightly coloured bag of chocolates. I didn't read the label as I rarely pay any attention to minor details like that. I came back into the training room and laid one piece of chocolate on each chair. When my students returned they were curious about the chocolates and picked them up and were unwrapping them slowly. In my normal fashion, I had unwrapped mine and eaten it very fast without really noticing much about it. I then became aware of some of my students saying how much they were enjoying the sensation of the chocolate 'popping' in their mouths. I wondered what they meant and picked up the now empty bag. It said something like 'champagne chocolates – put them on your tongue and enjoy the fizz'.

Sometimes the biggest lessons come in the smallest examples. I wondered what there was for me to learn from that experience and I realised that I rushed through my life in search of my goals without savouring each step of the journey. It was one of the most important lessons I made that year and it helped me to slow down and enjoy living in the now. The next day one of my students bought another bag of the same chocolates and this time I just put mine into my mouth and enjoyed the sensation as it literally sizzled on my tongue.

The power of values

I spoke in Chapter 3 of the importance of our values in the context of my career change. We're going to explore them in more detail now. Our values determine how we spend our time. They are the reason that we do what we do. They motivate us to take action and they are the means by which we evaluate ourselves after the event, and decide if we did a good job – or, indeed, the right thing. Our values also provide our moral code, so if we feel uncomfortable about anything we've done it's likely to be due to a conflict of values. Yet, they are largely unconscious. As a result, we may unknowingly choose goals that are not aligned to our values. When this happens we often experience an inner conflict between what is going on around us and how we feel on the inside. This can then manifest as unhappiness or an illness. So it's really important to find out now how far your goals are aligned to your values.

Aligning your values to your goals

I'm going to show you a powerful process that you can use to discover your values in relation to your goals. If your values are aligned to your goals, it will become much easier to achieve them as you'll naturally feel motivated and willing to do whatever it takes to achieve them.

Exercise 13

My values in relation to my goals

When eliciting values it's best to find someone who can work with you to ask you the questions. Choose a friend who can act as your coach. One of the rules of this exercise is to ask them to keep going with the questioning, even when your answers dry up. This is because your conscious values come out first, as they are at surface level. Your unconscious values are those that you are least aware of, and are likely to come out later and may prove to be the most important of all the values you identify.

Step 1: elicitation

Get your exercise partner to ask you the following question: 'What's important to you about achieving your goals?' By the way, these should be goals in general and not necessarily the goals you set back in Exercise 5. That's because we're going to check out those goals against your values later in this exercise to ensure that they are fully aligned.

Your partner must write down the words that you say and not suggest any answers, as these are their own values, not yours. In NLP, the words we are listening for are called 'nominalisations'. These are abstract nouns, i.e. they don't refer to objects in the real world. For example, the word 'mountain' is an object that we can see and touch. The word 'responsibility' is a noun that doesn't refer to an object that we can see or touch, and is therefore a nominalisation. Also, listen out for answers such as 'meeting new people'. This is not a nominalisation. In these cases your partner should ask: 'What does meeting new people do or get for you in relation to your goals?' You might then say: 'It gives me personal growth'. Personal growth then is the value.

Here is an example to help you get the idea. When you are asked what is important to you about your goals, you say in quick succession:

- making a difference
- security
- learning
- fame
- fortune
- independence
- flexibility
- variety.

You then say 'visiting new places'. This is not a value, so your partner asks you: 'What does visiting new places do or get for you?' You say 'fun'. This is the value. Add 'fun' to your list.

- making a difference
- security
- learning
- fame
- fortune
- independence
- flexibility
- variety
- fun.

You then say you can't think of any more. That means you are at the end of the first wave. Your partner carries on, asking 'What is important to you about achieving your goals?' to discover your second wave or those values held at a more unconscious level.

You then say:

- inspiration
- legacy

- personal growth
- authenticity
- permanence.

So, five more values are identified from the second wave.

Here is the list so far:

- making a difference
- security
- learning
- fame
- fortune
- independence
- flexibility
- variety
- fun
- inspiration
- legacy
- personal growth
- authenticity
- permanence.

Step 2: hierarchy of values

Your exercise partner should now give you the list of values and ask you to pick the top eight, and then rank them in order of priority. This may seem a challenge, and yet it is important to understand the most important through to the least important.

Step 3: re-write your list

Your exercise partner should then re-write your list in the order you have given. You may find that some of your most important values came out in the second wave of elicitation. This is quite common and means that some of your most important values were those held at an unconscious level.

Let's assume that this is the final list in our example:

1. inspiration
2. legacy
3. security
4. fame
5. variety
6. fun
7. personal growth
8. authenticity.

You'll notice that inspiration and legacy from the second wave are now at numbers 1 and 2 on the list, demonstrating the importance of carrying on with the questioning.

Step 4: test

You may feel that your values are in the right order. However, your exercise partner should check them as follows. Your partner starts with value number 1 (the most important) and asks (using our example): 'Assuming you could have inspiration (value number 1) but not legacy (value number 2), would that be OK with you?'

They need to force a choice from you. If you say it is OK, then those values are in the right order. If you say it's not OK, the values need to be reversed – in other words, number 2 becomes number 1 and vice versa. Your partner then checks value number 2 against number 3 until you get to the end of the eight values. You can then be sure that they are in the right order.

Step 5: how do your goals stack up?

Now go back to your goals in Exercise 5. We're going to evaluate them against your values. You may need to take one goal at a time or take the one that will have the biggest impact on your life first. Go through your list of eight values and score your current goal out of 10 against each value. See the hypothetical example opposite for guidance.

1. inspiration   9/10
2. legacy   10/10
3. security   6/10
4. fame   8/10
5. variety   8/10
6. fun   4/10
7. personal growth   9/10
8. authenticity   10/10

I normally break the scores into three categories:

0–4	High-risk area
5–7	Medium-risk area
8–10	Low-risk area for the relationship.

In our example, the two highest values are a low-risk area for the goal. However, in the longer-term security and fun are likely to be serious challenges to this goal. Unless this goal can be adjusted to bring both security and fun, the level of this person's motivation is likely to diminish over time.

Ask yourself where are the high- and medium-risk areas for you? Go back to your goal and work out what needs to change to bring your alignment to 100 per cent.

Other tips about values

Notice if any of the values that you elicited were phrased as a negative. For example, 'not being poor'. In NLP, this is an example of what is called an 'away-from' value. That's because you are moving away from what you don't want as opposed to moving towards what you want. In contrast, 'having abundance' is a 'towards' value. Both of these examples will create motivation for you. However, the motivation is fundamentally different. 'Away from' motivation doesn't feel good and there is the danger that when you focus on what you don't want, i.e., not being poor, that's what you'll get (remember Chapter 4 – focus on what you want).

The problem is that 'away from' motivation is not consistent. For example, if one of your values is 'not being poor', you will take massive action to earn some money. Once you have money again, your motivation drops and the money stops coming in. You then become very motivated again and go out and earn money. However, it's a 'boom and bust' mentality that isn't stable in the longer term. In contrast, 'towards' values have much more consistent and long-term motivation. 'Away from' values are created during significant emotional experiences – for example, if your parents went bankrupt, you may create a new 'away from' value of not wanting to be poor. These are created at an unconscious level so you are not necessarily aware of them consciously until you work through a process like the one in this book. To change these you need to become consciously aware of them first. As I've said already, awareness is a vital first step. Then ask yourself, what there is for you to learn from that 'away from' value. How is it specific to you, positive and for the future? This will make it easier to let the negative experience go. Go back and make sure that all your values in this exercise are towards values.

Now you know the process for eliciting values, use this exercise on other core areas of your life such as career, health and fitness and your intimate relationship. Remember, elicit your values for your ideal career, level of fitness, relationship, etc., not the way you do or have it now. Then compare your current job, level of fitness, intimate relationship to what is most important to you. You may be surprised with what you discover!

Pulling it altogether

This chapter is all about personal leadership and personal awareness. To be able to change your life and create what you want, it's vital to know yourself first. That's why in the corporate leadership programmes I design and run, we begin by running several self-assessment exercises. Awareness teaches you about your strengths that you can mobilise to really support you in your journey. You also learn about those traits that might potentially hold you back. In this chapter we've learned about our meta programmes, communication styles and values. You now know much more about your own personality than at the start. Check out what you have learned with those close to you to get feedback on the level of accuracy. You might even get those closest to you to complete the evaluations as well to see if you are aligned with each other in the pursuit of what you want. The biggest difference when you have everything in alignment with your goals is that creating change will start to feel easy. So it's worth doing then, isn't it?

Tip: Remember that your meta programmes, communication styles and values are your filters through which you experience the world. Start to change them and your world will also shift.

Chapter

'Every cause has its effect, every effect has its cause;
everything happens according to law. Chance is but a
name for law not recognised.'

From *The Kybalion*

Results or excuses? Taking responsibility for what you really want

What is it that makes the difference between two successful people? What makes one world class and the other good? This is the question that perplexed Richard Bandler and John Grinder, the creators of the body of knowledge we know as NLP. They made it their life's work to discover the answers. One of the ways they went about doing this was to find world-class models of excellence and to find out how they did what they did. One of the key findings was concerned with what can be described as the 'mindset for success'. How do successful people create their model of the world, and how is it different from other people's? Successful people do not have fewer problems than unsuccessful people, but they *do* deal with problems in a different way. It's not 'luck' that separates successful people from those who never make it; it's about how they perceive a situation and how they respond to what happens. It is this that makes the difference. This is one of the most important chapters in this book because it will show you how to apply this knowledge to your own life.

Consider for a moment. How do you live your life? Do you experience your life as hard and difficult or do you generally look on the positive side of life? I'm sure you are familiar with the 'glass half empty/glass half full' way of seeing the world. What about you? What is your starting point, your point of view? Some people will only see problems in a situation whereas others always see the opportunity. Are you someone who blames others or circumstances for whatever happens or are you someone who takes responsibility for whatever happens to you in your life? Does this sound familiar to you? For example, do you recognise yourself as someone who says 'Yes, I'd like to but...' or are you the person who says, 'Yes, let's go for it!'? Are you buffeted by events, feeling out of control, disempowered, a victim? Or are you involved, interested and active in what you do? In NLP terms, this is called either living life at **effect or at cause.**

Living your life at effect

If you are *at effect,* you will blame others or circumstances for your bad moods or for what you have not achieved, or for your life in general. You will feel disempowered and will depend on others in order to feel good about yourself or about life. 'If only my partner, my boss, my colleagues, my parents, my children... understood me and helped me achieve my dreams or did what I wanted or what is best for me, then life would be great, etc.' If you wait and hope for things to be different or for others to provide for your well-being, you are at effect or a victim of circumstances. And really, how much fun is that? And how much fun do you think it is for others to be around someone like you who is always moaning about their problems?

Believing that someone else is responsible, or making them responsible, for your happiness or your different moods is very limiting and gives that other person some mystical power over you, which can cause you a great deal of pain. No one can 'make' us do or feel anything. We react to someone else's behaviour and we have a choice about how we react. For example, if I hear one of my clients saying something like, 'He makes me sad', I'll ask them, 'How is his behaviour causing you to choose to be sad?' This puts the person back at cause where they have choices about how they react and behave. People at effect give away their power because they always look outside themselves for the solution. Those who live their lives at effect often see themselves or live their lives as victims because they believe they have no choices. The irony is that they do have choice and they have chosen not to choose but to be responsive to whatever is given to them. What does this remind you of? People in the Grey Zone tend to be at effect because they do not believe it's possible to live their lives in any other way.

Tom – it's not my fault

Tom had been going for interviews for new jobs and had had 11 interviews in the past 3 months. He was frustrated because he kept being turned down. When he described the interviews to me one thing really stuck out in his language. It was never his fault – he was unwell, the interview panel were against him from the start, there was an internal candidate, he was asked the wrong questions. The list was endless. Because it was never his fault, he didn't reflect on what he had learnt (his 'learnings' as we call them) from each interview. He was 'at the effect' of his interview experiences. His challenge was how to move to the cause side of the scenario and begin to take responsibility for what was really going on.

Living your life at cause

Alternatively, being at *cause* of what goes on around you forms the foundation of the 'mindset for success'. It's a common thread throughout personal development books. The first of Stephen Covey's seven habits in *The 7 Habits of Highly Effective People* is to be 'proactive'. He talks about being proactive as taking responsibility for everything in life. Sounds familiar, doesn't it? In *Unlimited Power*, Tony Robbins says that whatever happens, take responsibility. He says that, 'Achievers believe that no matter what happens, whether it's good or bad, they created it.'

I do not believe that it's coincidental that you hear the same viewpoint over and over again. Successful leaders talk about being **at cause** in one form or another, although they may give it another title or name.

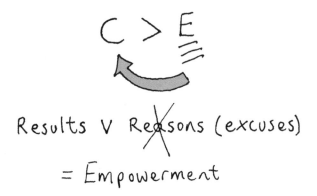

The *Kybalion*, published back in 1908, contains the seven Hermatic principles of success. These principles were adapted from ancient Egyptian and Greek wisdom. The principle of cause and effect embodies the fact that there is a cause for every effect that happens. This implies that there is no such thing as chance and that nothing merely happens.

In modern-day terms, being at cause means that you are decisive in creating what you want in life and you take responsibility for whatever happens – good or bad. You see the world as a place of opportunity and you move towards achieving what you want. If things are not happening as you would like, you take action and explore other possibilities. Above all, you know you have **choice** in what you do and how you react to people and events.

Simon – staying in the ring

Simon had been in a relationship for many years and had two grown-up daughters. His relationship had gone stale because neither partner had been prepared to put in the investment of time and energy to keep the magic going. They both found it easier to blame each other rather than take personal responsibility for changing things. He began to have frequent affairs as that seemed the only way to bring the excitement back into his life. As the deceit and lies grew, he became depressed and lost the sparkle for life. He was in the Awful Zone and his wife threatened to leave him. He focused on what they both needed to make the relationship a success and took 100 per cent personal responsibility for doing whatever it took to get things back on track. His wife agreed to give it a final go. He found himself communicating with his wife more than he had done in years in order to work out what was important to both of them about the relationship. Things began to improve and they have just moved to France and celebrated their twenty-fifth wedding anniversary.

Questions are the answer

People at cause live their lives in a different way. Essentially, they challenge themselves with a different set of questions. These questions are also great for assisting others to move to the cause side of life. Whatever happens in their lives, those at cause ask themselves:

**How have I managed to create this in my life
and for what purpose?**

The power of this is that if you ask yourself a different question you'll get a different answer. When I ask myself and my clients this question it's amazing what pops into their minds to give them a new and empowering perspective on their situation. These answers often come directly from our unconscious minds. People at cause empower themselves because they keep hold of the problem. They do not give away the opportunity to find a solution by blaming others. You see, if you keep the problem inside yourself, then you will always have the opportunity to find a solution. Are you with me on this? This is the most **empowering** way to lead your life. Being at cause means that you have choices in your life. For example, if you are in a relationship that's not working for you and you blame the other person, because in your model of the world they never do anything right, you are likely to stay stuck in the Grey Zone and remain miserable. If, however, you are at cause, you take responsibility for the relationship, and if it's not working, you know you have the choice to do something different. There's always a choice for people at cause, whereas when you are at effect, it often feels like you have no choice.

People at cause take more decisions than most people because they are always proactively searching out a new solution. The law of averages dictates that not all will work out well. However, people at cause ask themselves another great question. Instead of beating themselves up when things don't go exactly to plan, they ask:

What could I do differently next time?

This focuses them on trying something else next time instead of on what they did wrong. I've noticed that many of my coaching clients get stuck in the same old behaviour loop. They believe if something isn't working well, the solution is to do more of it. They invest more time and money in something that is already proven not to work. They become like the hamster in the hamster wheel, running faster and faster and getting nowhere. Madness. I like to say:

If you always do what you've always done you always get what you've always got.

I have met a woman who says this mantra quite literally changed her life, and it'll change yours too. Asking 'What could I do differently next time?' helps you to break out of the old behavioural patterns.

Sally – doing something different

One of my clients was getting very frustrated because she really fancied someone. He was the father of her son's best friend. He was unattached, good looking, well dressed and had a great job. She is an attractive woman and had always found it easy in the past to get noticed by men. But not this particular one... and he wasn't gay. She worked on every trick in the book – wearing sexy clothes, turning up in all the places she knew he'd be, finding excuses to call him to invite his son over to play, asking him in for coffee when he arrived to collect his son. Nothing worked. Exasperated, she asked me for a coaching session. I listened to her story and had only one thing to say to her. Do something different! All her usual strategies for attracting men were not having any impact so it was time for drastic action. She asked me what to do and I gave her my normal advice in these situations – do the opposite of what you're doing now. This is usually a good place to start. So she took my advice and began to ignore this guy completely. She dressed normally around him and stopped the coffees. It wasn't long before he was calling her to find out if she was OK. In fact, he asked her out to dinner to see if she was OK – she said 'no' the first time but eventually she went. The rest is history, as they say!

In my view, it almost doesn't matter what you do as long as you take action that is in some way aligned to your goal. I say this because if you take action, learn from it and change your approach accordingly, you will create the momentum to get the result that you want in the end.

In NLP there is a series of presuppositions or assumptions upon which NLP is based. They provide us with a great guide about how to lead your life to empower not only yourself but also those around you. One of these is:

There is no failure, only feedback.

This means that whenever things don't go to plan, you do not focus on what went wrong or think of it as a failure. Instead you ask yourself another great question, which ensures that 'you get the learnings' from the situation so that you can move on faster and not create the same pattern another time:

What is there to learn from this experience?

The truly amazing thing about learnings is that when you get them I guarantee that it is possible to let go of the past and to move on. This way of thinking allows us to let things go and move on much quicker than most of the population, who often remain stuck in the past. When we talk about learnings, they must come in a particular format for them to work.

Learnings are always:

- for you personally
- positive
- for the future.

Fundamentally, learnings are for yourself because you cannot control someone else's behaviour. They are what you *will* do differently in future, not what you shouldn't or won't do again – as we know from Chapter 4 this will focus your attention in the wrong direction. They are always for the future as the past has already happened. So, a learning at the end of a relationship might be, 'I will learn to enjoy life, spending time by myself as well as with others in future', as opposed to, 'I'm miserable unless I'm spending time with my partner'. Got it?

I confess that living life at cause can sometimes feel more of a challenge than living life at effect. It sometimes feels this way because you are placing new demands on yourself – because your action is to do something differently – view this is a good thing. In fact, life becomes far less stressful because you always know there is a choice and you are freed up from relying on excuses. And, if you want to move out of the Grey Zone, this is the way to run your life. With this mindset you cannot not achieve the goals that you set for yourself, because you take responsibility for what you want, you are flexible and when things do not go to plan you get the learnings, move on quickly and take a different approach next time.

You now have an opportunity to live your life at cause for one month. At first, if you're not sure what to do, just pretend – act 'as if'. Enjoy the experience and reflect on your learnings.

Exercise 14

Living life at the 'C side'

For the next month act *as if* you are at cause in your universe. Take responsibility for everything that happens to you. Ask yourself how you chose to create situations in your world and for what purpose. Find out what there is to learn from each situation and let it go.

Remember – ask yourself a different question and you get a different answer.

Write down your learnings from living life at cause:

The results v reasons model

In life you get one of two things:

THE RESULT YOU WANT

OR

LOADS OF REASONS WHY YOU DIDN'T GET YOUR RESULT.

This is what is known as the *'results v reasons' model*. Those at the cause side of the scenario are focused on their results. Those on the effect side are focused on finding enough reasons to let themselves off the hook. What are reasons? They are another word for **excuses**. An excuse will always follow the word 'but'. For example, 'I'd love to set up my own business but I don't know enough.' Excuses keep you in the Grey Zone. They keep you comfortable. The irony is that if you create enough excuses for not getting your result, you still walk away proudly slapping yourself on the back. How bizarre is that?

I remember holding a workshop with some very senior armed services' personnel. All the participants were men and I was in the process of explaining the results v reasons model when I noticed a brigadier on the front table becoming increasingly red in the face. In the end, he could contain himself no longer. He politely put up his hand and said to me: 'But Lindsey, in the Services we have very good reasons!'

It doesn't matter whether the reasons are seen to be good or not. At the end of the day, you either get your result or your reasons/excuses. There is no middle path. No one can take responsibility for your change except for you. I can be your tour guide but you have to take the journey. For example, on my NLP programmes, participants regularly expect to be 'fixed' by me. They often get disgruntled when they realise they have to *do* something different if they want something different.

Healing our lives

If we believe we are the creators of our own universe then we will be motivated to keep going and do something different if we don't at first get the result we want in our lives. I believe we can use the 'cause and effect' as a model for all areas of our lives and across all experiences, including illness.

I believe that disease can be a metaphor for what is happening in our emotional bodies. The type of illness often represents the significant emotional experience that the person is going through at the time. Our thoughts impact on our bodies so this is not surprising. If you can discover the trigger for the disease and heal it, the illness may spontaneously disappear. I know that it sounds far fetched but I have witnessed so many examples of this that I believe it does happen. Here's just one powerful example.

Sonja's story

Sonja had experienced deafness from an early age. She wore hearing aids in both ears. During a breakthrough session she was asked what it was that she didn't want to hear in her life. Sure enough, she had been influenced by a series of domineering men – first her father, then her brothers and then her husband. She wanted to break free and didn't know how. The really interesting thing was that she said that she loved to go alone to the cinema, and when in the cinema she took out her hearing aids and could hear. When asked why she loved the cinema so much, she answered that it was because there she got some peace away from her normal day-to-day surroundings – and, of course, the domineering men in her life. The process of the breakthrough session enabled her to move to the cause side of the equation by understanding why she might have chosen to create this problem that looked like deafness and for what purpose. By answering the questions in this chapter she was assisted to get the personal learnings. Using another technique called Time Line Therapy™, developed by Tad James in the 1980s, she was assisted in releasing the unconscious decision that she made at a young age to become deaf. Of course, we do not make these decisions consciously – that would be crazy. And, our unconscious minds have a habit of creating situations to solve problems for us. This woman was bullied by the men in her life and so her unconscious mind protected her by allowing her not to hear in every situation except the cinema.

At the end of the session she courageously removed her hearing aids to find she could hear again. I witnessed the whole thing with my own eyes. Her close friend and travelling companion was a doctor and he couldn't believe what he had seen. It was also a wonderful convincer for everyone involved of the power of the mind and of the power of being at cause in your universe.

Tip: Be at cause in everything you do and notice the magic in life as nothing is left to chance or to others to achieve on your behalf.

Chapter 7

'No one can make you feel inferior
without your consent.'

Eleanor Roosevelt

Believe you can

We know from Chapter 4 how important it is to focus on what we want to achieve. There is another important dimension to this. If you were to adopt all the principles in this book so far, i.e. setting goals, focusing on what you want, living life at cause, would that be enough to guarantee you success? Well, it depends on what you believe about yourself. For example, what would happen if I went after my goal to set up my own company? I focus on my success, I take responsibility for everything that happens in my life. All good so far. Yet, if at an unconscious level I believe that people in my family are never going to be achievers, what will that do to me? As our beliefs shape what we believe to be possible, my belief will eventually lead to incongruence with my goal. In some way I will end up sabotaging my results. I'm likely to delete the many potential opportunities that come my way because my belief leads me to run a pattern that says it's meant to be really hard or even impossible for me to achieve my success.

I'm constantly amazed at the number of companies that put their staff through a training programme and expect that programme to have a lasting impact on their people. For example, a salesperson sent on a course to improve their sales skills will learn new tools and techniques. This may affect their behaviour in the short term, yet it's often short-lived. Why? Because, if at some level they believe they are never going to be a brilliant salesperson, that will limit the impact of the training. They may do better for a while and then their limiting beliefs about themselves begin to creep back in. Are you with me so far on this? As it is vital on our journey to focus on what we want in our lives, to understand our own belief system and the impact of this on our goals, you will need to change your beliefs so that your goals and beliefs are totally aligned. I'll show you how.

What are beliefs?

Our beliefs are views about ourselves, other people and situations that we hold to be true. They are emotionally held views not based on fact. They are feelings of certainty that we have about something. For example, if you believe you are fit, what you're actually saying is that you have a feeling of certainty that you are fit. Alternatively, if you have lack of belief or, in other words, a limiting belief that you are fit, it is likely to hold you back.

Morris Massey, a sociologist, in his book *People Puzzle – Understanding Yourself*, describes the imprint period between the ages of 0 and 7 as the moment when our beliefs are formed. They are shaped by key people in our lives at that time, for example parents, teachers, religious leaders, close family, etc. In actual fact, most of our beliefs are generalisations that we create from life experiences. Most of us do not consciously decide what we will believe; most of us are generously donated our beliefs by influential parent figures during our imprint period, and once we have a belief we forget that it can be changed and it becomes our reality. We rarely challenge our long-held beliefs and they become a filter through which we sieve all our life's expectations and experiences.

Bridgit – awareness is the first step to recovery

Bridgit had set up her own business but, despite some successes, the company was not yet reaching its potential and she was dangerously close to having to close it down. She came to me for a breakthrough session as she couldn't understand why success was proving to be elusive and such hard work when it did come to her. During her session I did some work with her on her limiting beliefs. It became clear during questioning that her parents were very religious and in fact they had always had a very different view to her about money. They believed money to be the root of all evil and this was often discussed in front of my client and her brothers and sisters. Consequently, whenever she got close to making money with her company she would unconsciously sabotage the process. Once I helped her to become more aware of what was going on, she could begin to challenge and change that old belief. It became OK for her to make money and she doubled her turnover of the previous year in the next three months.

How do we create beliefs?

When I think of beliefs I have a metaphor in my mind of a new house being built with basic building blocks being put on top of a foundation. From the example above, 'money is the root of all evil' would be the foundation of the belief which was generated by a commonly held view in that family. We then begin to collect building blocks or 'reference experiences', as coined by Tony Robbins, to support that foundation. The more building blocks we add, the stronger the belief becomes. My client began to filter information according to the belief that 'money is the root of all evil'. Her building blocks were each an example of where this belief had been reinforced by an experience that she had seen, heard, felt and so on. For example, other people supported the idea, a TV programme, an article in the paper, a book, a film. It didn't take long before her reticular activating system was only bringing to her attention evidence that the belief was true. Her RAS acted as a pair of 'money is the root of all evil' tinted glasses. Other opportunities to see money in a different light were missed as they were outside her awareness. Once the belief was changed, she then began to notice new opportunities coming her way easily and effortlessly.

Our beliefs are often held in the deepest levels of our unconscious mind. They are strongly influenced by the behaviour of the significant people in our lives, frequently our parents, before the age of seven. One way to unravel your limiting beliefs is to reflect on your parents' attitude to relationships, money, sex, etc. You may be unconsciously modelling them or rebelling against their behaviour.

Limiting beliefs about ourselves act as a self-fulfilling prophecy. We know this from our discussions in Chapter 4 about getting what you focus on. If our beliefs are limiting us we act in a way that proves our beliefs to ourselves. However, if we have empowering beliefs we act and behave in a way that releases our potential and allows us to be our true selves. Let's look at the impact of our beliefs on our thoughts and our actions with the example of 'getting fit'.

Example 1

Belief

- I can't get fit.

Outcome

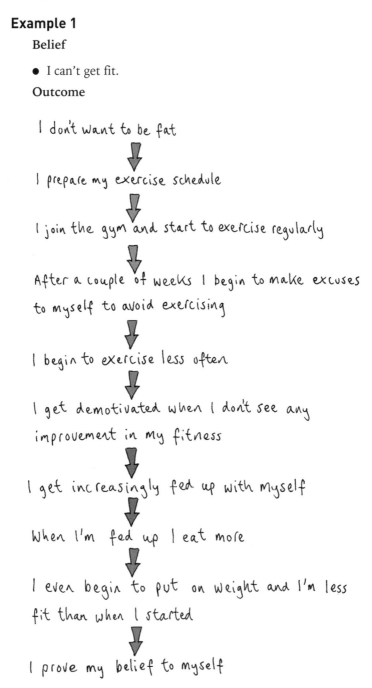

I don't want to be fat

I prepare my exercise schedule

I join the gym and start to exercise regularly

After a couple of weeks I begin to make excuses to myself to avoid exercising

I begin to exercise less often

I get demotivated when I don't see any improvement in my fitness

I get increasingly fed up with myself

When I'm fed up I eat more

I even begin to put on weight and I'm less fit than when I started

I prove my belief to myself

Example 2

Belief

- I believe I can get fit easily.

Outcome

I have a vision of how great I will look and feel when I'm fit

⬇

I prepare my exercise schedule

⬇

I join the gym and start to exercise regularly

⬇

I feel excited and motivated as I notice my body shape changing

⬇

I notice my weight starting to reduce

⬇

I feel good about myself and look forward to showing off the new me

⬇

I buy myself some new clothes to reward myself

⬇

I continue to get fitter

⬇

I reach my target fitness and weight

⬇

I prove my belief to myself

Which cycle are you on at the moment? Do you spend your time focusing on your empowering or limiting beliefs about yourself?

The power of our beliefs

Another dimension to the importance of beliefs is their potential impact on our health and ageing process. *In Ageless Body, Timeless Mind*, Deepak Chopra wrote that people grow old and die because they see others grow old and die. Norman Cousins, who developed 'laughter therapy', proposed that 'belief creates biology'. Our inherited expectation is that our body will wear out over time and that we are destined to suffer, grow old and die. Chopra estimates that, without negative influences from outside, our bodies could last between 115 and 130 years before the ageing process finally caused them to shut down.

The Tarahumara people in Mexico are an interesting example of what can happen when a tribe lives away from the rest of society and outside influences. There are about 40,000 of them scattered in small villages across remote mountains and canyons. Their name for themselves is 'Rarámuri' or foot runners. Running has always been a central part of their culture as it's the only way for them to get around. In 1993, Victoriano Churro won the ultramarathon, the Leadville Trail 100. This is the most gruelling marathon in the US because nearly all of the race is run at elevations of 10,000 feet. He ran in sandals made of leather thongs and nails. The interesting thing is that Victoriano was 55 when he won the race. The Tarahumara believe that runners do not reach their prime until they are approaching 60 and this is what they create in their tribe. The best runners in the tribe are in their late 50s and 60s.

This is in complete contrast to the Western model. In fact, in the UK and the US, mandatory retirement is set at age 65. After this date you are no longer socially useful and you become one of society's dependants. Medically, the impact of this perception shift can be disastrous. Chopra talks of 'early retirement death' where, in the first few years after retirement, heart attacks and cancer rates soar. Maybe time for us to consider moving to Mexico!

Carol – stepping into what is possible

Throughout the ages firewalking has been practised for emotional and physical healing and renewal. Carol wanted to get herself back on track after a difficult divorce. Her self-esteem and confidence were at an all-time low. She was searching for a way of regaining her personal power. She was the last to walk that evening, believing it to be impossible and terrified of burning her feet. Even after watching others walk safely she was still hesitant. I asked her to consider how walking the fire would change her beliefs about every area of her life. How powerful would you feel after walking across fire? There was not a dry eye in the group as Carol walked successfully and painlessly across the fire. It had represented the barrier to her moving on and now that was gone. I watched her go from strength to strength after that night and she now has a new relationship and a fulfilling new life.

Just imagine if you were to do something that you thought was impossible. What impact would that have on all other areas of your life?

How do we change beliefs?

Changing beliefs is absolutely possible and necessary if change is to stick. For example, when I teach somebody presentation skills, I work at a number of levels. Students learn new skills and behaviours but that isn't enough. They also need to believe that they are a great presenter. If they do not build new beliefs about being a great presenter, the danger is that the limiting belief about themselves as a presenter will sabotage their new behaviours, skills and capabilities. That is why so many organisations have wasted millions of pounds on training programmes that only train at the level of behaviour and skill.

This also fits for our goals. If you set a goal for yourself that is not in alignment with your beliefs, how successful do you think you will be in achieving it? For example, your goal is to set up your own business and you have researched everything thoroughly. You have the skills and capabilities to be successful. However, you believe at a deep unconscious level that you are not good enough to have what you want. What impact will that have on your goal? That's right, it will eventually sabotage your focus.

Exercise 15

Changing what you believe

Step 1

The first step is to find out your limiting and empowering beliefs about yourself. Some of these you'll be consciously aware of. Write those down first. Then think of situations that have held you back in life and situations where you have been successful. Consider why that has been – what was the difference in your beliefs? Go with whatever pops into your mind. Think about this especially in connection with your goal.

Examples of limiting beliefs:

● Negations – for example, I'm not capable, I can't make money, I'm too old, I don't believe I can do..., etc.

● Comparatives – for example, I'm not good enough.

My disempowering beliefs

Now write down your empowering beliefs about yourself. Connect again with your goal and consider what beliefs will really support you on your journey.

Examples of empowering beliefs:

- I'm good at what I do.
- People like me.
- I'm a confident person.

My empowering beliefs

Step 2

Then circle the three most influential disempowering and empowering beliefs on your lists. Consider first how your empowering beliefs can strengthen your life even more than they do now. Write down specific examples of how your empowering beliefs are working in your life right now:

- Empowering belief 1

- Empowering belief 2

- Empowering belief 3

Step 3

Ask yourself what it will cost you in your life if you do not let go of your limiting beliefs in terms of your goals, your health, your wealth and your relationships. Write down the answers below and be honest with yourself. Associate your-self into the feelings of the cost of not changing. Do this by imagining yourself in five years' time – what impact will these limiting beliefs have had on your life?

What my limiting beliefs are costing me/will cost me:

That wasn't pleasant, was it? It wasn't meant to be. Tony Robbins says that if we associate enough pain with anything, we'll change. You may find that your limiting beliefs have already been seriously eroded by completing this exercise.

Step 4

Take each of your three limiting beliefs in turn and list all the evidence you can think of as to why they are not actually true. For example, if you believe that you'll never be successful, write down what you'd like to believe instead – e.g. I am successful – and then list all the times you have been successful so far. Remember, you will have been wearing your 'I'm not successful tinted glasses' up until now. Think carefully and dig deep into your unconscious mind for the answers. This is the time to change. Find as many new building blocks as possible.

My limiting belief is:

My new belief is:

My new building blocks are:

- ....
  ....
- ....
  ....
- ....
  ....

My limiting belief is:

My new belief is:

My new building blocks are:

- ....
  ....
- ....
  ....
- ....
  ....

My limiting belief is:

My new belief is:

My new building blocks are:

- ....
  ....
- ....
  ....
- ....
  ....

Well done! Keep focusing on your new beliefs and building new building blocks for yourself as this is your evidence that the belief has changed, and you will be surprised how you begin to experience the world differently now.

Other ways of changing beliefs

I've also experienced other ways of changing beliefs that I'd like to share with you. These are the more impromptu events. For example, sometimes someone can say something to you that completely changes the meaning or the context of your thought. In NLP we call it 'reframing'. In an instant it can change our beliefs for ever.

There was a time when I was procrastinating about setting up my company. I had registered the name of The Change Corporation and I had run some pilot NLP programmes in my own time. I just needed to hand in my resignation and get on with it. Yet, despite all my skills and capabilities, I wasn't taking the action I needed to take. It wasn't happening because I still didn't believe I was up to it. I was hearing myself making loads of excuses about delaying the date even further. Most of all I was terrified of jumping off the cliff and having to fly by myself. Two of my closest friends decided that they would take me away to France for my birthday. My friends were rather secretive and I thought it was about my birthday present but I was wrong. At my birthday lunch in a seafront hotel I discovered they had actually lured me there to give me a good talking to! We had a great lunch with lots of chilled champagne while watching the ocean. It was a perfect afternoon. Then both my friends started to ask me about my plans for the next year and began to challenge me about why I had not yet left my job. I began to get irritated with them and started to switch off my attention and look away around the room.

Then all of a sudden, one of my friends asked me a question:

"Is the name of your company The Change Corporation or The Stay as You Are Corporation?**"**

In an instant she had my attention. I began to laugh out loud as I realised that she had just given me one of the most exquisite reframes that I had ever heard. They had me! I went from angry to frustrated to tears of laughter in a few seconds. The next day back at work in London, I handed in my notice and I was on my way. My limiting beliefs about myself had been reframed in an instant.

What if you were to align your beliefs to your goal right now. What impact would that have on you? What would it really be like for you? I guarantee that your journey towards your goal will suddenly feel easier. Being totally congruent you would soon notice new opportunities that had passed you by before. Your goal would feel like a certainty for the first time in your life. What would it feel like to go out into the future and look back having made those changes? What will you look like, feel like and sound like believing in yourself for maybe the first time in your life? It's totally possible and you have to take the first step and be honest with yourself about what has held you back until now. If you've not yet completed the exercise on changing your beliefs go back and enjoy changing the tinted glasses you've been wearing up until now.

Tip: We can never be more than we believe is possible, so start to believe in possibilities.

Chapter

8

'Passion is energy. Feel the passion by
focusing on what excites you.'

Oprah Winfrey

You have all you need to succeed

In this chapter we'll be exploring the inner resources we all have inside ourselves that are often left undiscovered and, therefore, untapped. Yet, these are the resources of **excellence** that will be invaluable to you as you take the first step towards doing something different with your life.

Another presupposition in NLP is that:

You have all the resources you need to succeed.

This is important because people make loads of excuses about why they cannot have what they truly want. The most common excuses are not having enough money or time, not feeling confident enough or not having the energy to achieve what they want. They look outside themselves for the answers. The most successful people, however, recognise that the place to look for more resources is within themselves. In this chapter we are going to explore how you can maximise your inner resources to get what you want. I'll show you how you can use your energy reserves more effectively, how time is an illusion for you to construct the way that works best for you and how you can control your emotions to feel good in an instant. I often meet people who are totally unaware of the choices they can make to increase their potential. Huge amounts of money are spent every day by people who want to feel good without them knowing that they can achieve this for themselves in an instant for **free**. In NLP we learn how to work with ourselves on an energetic level to harness and utilise our resources to the maximum. Let's begin that journey right now. Are you ready to experiment for a moment with your energy?

Exercise 16

Improve your focus, improve your results

You'll need to stand up to do this exercise. Find a space where you can move around with your arm outstretched freely. Look forwards and stand with your feet apart. Stand rooted to the floor. Keep your legs still, raise your right arm horizontally out in front of you and gently twist around keeping your arm horizontal until you cannot twist any further. Note carefully to yourself where your arm is pointing – maybe there's something in the room you can take as a marker. Or if you have someone else with you, ask them to stand as a marker for where your arm got to. Now focus behind you and find a spot beyond where your arm reached the first time. Fix that spot in your mind as you turn back around to face the front again. Twist again moving your arm as far as it will go. Hold it steady, turn around and see how much further you have moved your arm this time. You will find that you have moved your arm much further the second time around. You may have twisted to way beyond the point even you visualised.

This is a great example of the fact that your energy flows to where your attention goes. I did this exercise with a group of middle managers recently. One of them, from Singapore, thought this was the most illuminating exercise he could remember because it's a great metaphor for how we can always achieve a better result from within ourselves when we focus. The exercise demonstrates that a little more focus goes a long way – 10 per cent extra delivers more than 10 per cent in results. Normally, our energy is dissipated all over the place.

I'd like to show you how you can access the energy and feelings that you want, when you want them to gain control over your capacity and potential to do well, and I'll show you how you can make time work for you in future. Imagine right now how much difference that would make to your life.

The power of energy

❝The body is not what it seems to be with the naked eye. It is not a solid mass. It is actually a system of little particles or points of energy separated from each other by space and held in place through an electrically balanced field.❞ **David Cumes**

Energy is our life force and yet we act as if we have no control over it. I hear people saying they are having a 'low energy' day as if they have no control over their bodies.

Consider this scene. You arrive at your holiday destination in the South of France. You have been looking forward to it for months as you love the sun. It is pouring with rain and cold for the time of year. You are miserable. It's a low energy day. You begin to feel less than resourceful about your holiday. It's not fair. You have the worst holiday ever. Does that sound familiar? Remember that you get what you focus on.

Now consider this scene. You arrive at your holiday destination in the South of France. You have been looking forward to it for months as you love the sun. It is pouring with rain and cold for the time of year. You are full of anticipation of doing something new. As you can't sunbathe, you'll spend the trip exploring the countryside and learning about French food and wine. You've wanted to do that for years. You are full of energy. You have the best holiday ever. Does that sound familiar? Remember that you get what you focus on.

I'm sure that both scenarios will look, feel and sound familiar. The curious thing is that most people experience energy as something that happens to them. They are not in control. And yet, we can control our energy from moment to moment. I am reminded of a colleague who says that, whatever the weather, it's a brilliantly sunny day, or a brilliantly rainy day or a brilliantly windy day, etc. It's surprising what a difference that makes to your energy and how you feel. Some of the best fun I've had with my kids has been on days when it's been pouring with rain and we've been playing outside getting soaking wet. Just think what it would be like to be able to choose to feel that it's a brilliant day, every day, whatever the weather and whatever the situation.

The chakras – how we use energy in our bodies

The chakras are not, of course, from NLP, yet they give us the key to unlocking our energy to its full potential. Energy is the fuel of excellence. Think for a moment of your favourite car. Perhaps it's a beautiful sports car or an exciting 4 × 4. Whatever it is, imagine trying to drive it on the wrong fuel. It wouldn't work. It's the same for our bodies. To be at peak performance, we need to maximise our energy levels. The higher your energy level, the better you feel, and the better you feel, the more astounding your results will be. Our results are state dependent, as we already know. Our energy comes from our breath. What's the difference between someone who is alive and someone who has just died? The person who has just died will no longer be breathing. Breath carries life and energy through the body.

You can also feel other people's energies. In fact, you do it all the time. For instance, think of someone who makes you feel great every time you see them. Notice how you feel inside your-self as you think of this person. Now, compare that experience with the way you feel around someone who seems depressed. Does their energy 'bring you down'? You are sensing each per-son's energy. Your best sensing mechanism for other people's energies is often your own body and emotions. When we sense a person's energy, we are reacting to many subtle vibrations at once. Everything a person thinks and feels affects his or her 'vibration' or range of subtle frequencies. In fact, thoughts and emotions are part of the spectrum of subtle energies.

In China, energy is called 'chi', meaning life force. In India it's referred to as *prana* or *shakti*. In Japan, it's *ki*. In the Kalahari desert, the aboriginal Kung call it *num*. The concept of a radiant subtle energy and spirit underlying the physical world is almost universal. So is the idea that this energy can be harnessed for profound transformation and healing. More than two thousand years ago, the Chinese created acupuncture, a system that uses needles to influence the flow of chi through the body's energy meridians. In India, mystics have been transmitting prana or shakti from master to student, changing consciousness, for at least as long. The Kalahari Kung raise num through ecstatic all-night dances, in which they perform healings and receive visions. This radiant subtle energy flows through the body, ener-gising our seven energy centres, or our chakras. We can learn how to manage this energy for maximising our performance.

When we begin to take control of our energy, we have the opportunity to take control of our state or mood. That is the link between energy, chakras and NLP. Our seven chakras func-tion as pumps or valves, regulating the flow of energy through our energy system. The functioning of the chakras reflects decisions we make concerning how we choose to respond to conditions in our life. We open and close these valves when we decide what to think, what to feel and through which perceptual filter we choose to experience the world around us. For exam-ple, if we have positive thoughts, we feel good and our energy levels are higher. We have more energy and vitality to enjoy our day. The seven chakras are identified and located as follows:

- chakra seven: crown chakra
- chakra six: brow chakra
- chakra five: throat chakra
- chakra four: heart chakra
- chakra three: solar plexus or power chakra
- chakra two: sexual chakra
- chakra one: root chakra.

The chakras are not physical. They are aspects of consciousness in the same way that the auras are aspects of consciousness. The chakras are more dense than the auras but not as dense as the physical body. The chakras represent not only particular parts of your physical body, but also particular parts of your consciousness.

For example, when you feel tension in your consciousness, you feel it in the chakra associated with that part of your consciousness experiencing the stress, and in the parts of the physical body associated with that chakra. Where you feel the stress depends upon why you feel the stress. When the tension continues over a period of time, or to a particular level of intensity, the person may create a symptom at the physical level.

The chakras are thought to vitalise the physical body and to be associated with interactions of a physical, emotional and mental nature. They are considered loci of life energy, or prana or chi. The function of the chakras is to spin and draw in this universal life force energy to keep the spiritual, mental, emotional and physical health of the body in balance. You can learn to move your energy around your body. You will already have had experiences of using energy from one chakra more than another and experiencing how others use their energy around you. For example, if you operate from your sexual chakra, you will find that some people don't feel comfortable around you and that you may attract the wrong kind of people. Think of a time when you felt uncomfortable in the presence of someone who was using their sexual energy around you. We've all had that experience or, conversely, we've all enjoyed sexual attraction where we may have described the sexual energy between you and another person as 'chemistry'.

If you operate from your solar plexus or power chakra, you may notice that people take you on, you get into frequent arguments or even worse, fights. And again, think of a time when someone has used their power around you – it is uncomfortable.

How do you begin to use your chakras with more precision? The first step is to put your attention on to a certain part of your body as your energy will flow from and to that part. We are going to experiment with a few exercises so you can experience this for yourself. You will need a partner for these exercises. Have fun!

Exercise 17

Learning how to utilise your energy

With your partner decide who will go first. Whoever goes first will stand on one spot and put their attention on their left ear lobe and imagine all their energy moving to the top of their head or their crown chakra. Once you are focusing all your energy on your crown chakra, your partner will *gently* push you on the shoulder. You should both notice what you notice. It is likely that the person pushed will wobble all over the place.

This time the first person will focus all their energy on to their lower stomach, just below the navel. Imagine your legs feeling absolutely grounded with roots growing through the floor you are standing on. Then your partner will push you *gently* again. Notice the difference. How did you feel the second time around? You will have been rooted to the ground and much firmer.

Then repeat the exercise swapping over with your partner.

Now consider the next time you have a challeging meeting, presentation or a one to one session. Imagine how much stronger you will feel as you get yourself totally grounded before you tackle that situation. Practise regularly and see how you get on.

Exercise 18

Your arm your strength

This time stand in front of your partner and rest your right arm on their shoulder, palm up. Your arm should make contact with their shoulder around the wrist area. Your partner then clasps their hands together above your arm and pushes down gently. Your arm will move down easily.

Then repeat the exercise but this time imagine your arm like a fireman's hose, with energy flowing through it keeping it strong. Your partner clasps your arm again and pushes down and notices the difference. This time your arm is as solid as a rock just by using your imagination.

Then repeat with your partner. Notice how we can become stronger in an instant without overexerting ourselves. This is what happens when we read in the newspapers of a miracle happening where someone has lifted a car to rescue a child.

Exercise 19

Moving your energy outside

This time stand approximately 15 feet away from your partner facing each other. Imagine sucking in all your energy inside yourself. Really focus on that. Then get your partner to move towards you and stop when they feel your energy field. You should notice that they can get very close to you, maybe almost on top of you, before stopping.

This time stand again approximately 15 feet away from your partner facing each other. Imagine your energy is creating a force field outside you and around you. Push it out to around six feet away from you. Focus on that, and when you are ready ask your partner to move towards you, stopping when they feel your energy field. Your partner slowly moves forward and then stops when they feel your energy field. Your partner is likely to stop somewhere between three and six feet away from you.

Then repeat with your partner. Notice how you can use this to protect yourself from tough situations. Just imagine your energy outside, a boundary between you and the rest of the world. Or alternatively, notice how you can give people or groups an energetic 'hug' whilst you're working with them. Practise this and notice how it improves your level of rapport.

Exercise 20

Raising your game

You do not need a partner for this but it's fun to experiment together. This time we are going to learn how to raise our energy levels really fast. Breathe in and as you do so raise your arms in a circular movement above your head. Now imagine pushing that energy out as you blow out, bringing your arms down at the same time. Do this six times and every time imagine the energy building up in your body. Notice how differently you feel after six power breaths. How do you feel at the moment?

I often use this technique to bring my energy levels up before I walk into my training room or before I'm about to begin a presentation. It's great for changing your state and therefore your feelings in an instant.

So now you know how to start to get your energy to work for you and to support you in all that you do. It is a resource that has been dormant for too long. Make the most of it starting from **now!**

The power of time

Lady Jane Fellowes read this quote by the American poet Henry van Dyke at the funeral of Diana, Princess of Wales:

"Time is too slow for those who wait, too swift for those who fear, too long for those who grieve, too short for those who rejoice, but for those who love, time is eternity.**"**

One of the other great excuses in life is not having the time to do what you really want to do. No time to work on your goals whether it be going to the gym three times a week or working long hours to establish your new business. So often I hear people say that they would go after their goals but they don't have enough time. They are already too **busy** in their lives not focusing on what is really **important**.

Finding the **energy** to do all you need to do is the first step. You will then find that you can live life in a more balanced and vitalised way. You will be able to achieve more than other people that you know, and others will notice how much more vitality you have and how much younger you look and feel. Don't be surprised if your friends want to know what your secret is. That is the first step.

Remember that your energy flows where your attention goes, and one of the impacts of utilising your energy to the full is that you will want to maximise every moment of every day. You will want the time to be able to maximise every experience. I'm going to introduce you to a different understanding of time that means you can create the time it takes. I call this **time distortion.**

Anybody who has ever had a long-distance relationship will know all about time distortion. When you are together, the time literally seems to fly past. The time apart until the next meeting feels like an eternity. If the long-distance relationship ends, time 'settles down' and every day feels the same length again.

Deepak Chopra writes that Einstein's brilliant contribution to modern physics was the idea that linear time is superficial. It is not a straight-line process. Time seems to flow and move, seconds, minutes, hours, days, months and years pass by. Yet, this is all relative – it has no absolute value. Einstein replaced the idea of time with something much more fluid. With fluid time, it can speed up or slow down depending upon the context. He noted that spending a minute on a hot stove seems like an hour, whereas spending an hour with someone you love seems like a minute. The conclusion is that time depends upon the situation of the **observer.** As the observer, we have personal control over our experience of time. We hear ourselves say things like:

'I don't have time for that.'

'Time stands still.'

'Time flies by.'

'Time is running out.'

These statements say nothing about linear time measured by the clock. They do say a great deal about how we experience time inside our nervous system. These statements reflect a sense of self. Your attitude towards time reflects how you are as a person. For example, people who never have time are more likely to develop health problems. Subjective time is a powerful force as it changes behaviour, attitudes and beliefs.

Deadlines

Chopra says it is no coincidence that the word 'deadline' includes the word 'dead'! Do you notice that some people are far more sensitive to time pressure than others? Some people blossom, others feel under threat. In business, setting a tight deadline is often what I would describe as a 'macho' behaviour, with deadlines often set arbitrarily and often set earlier than is necessary. I experienced this many times at the consultancy company I worked for. Often the deadline for a project was agreed without consideration for the impact of the deadline on the project team required to deliver the work. And, there were times when the delivery team discovered that the client would have been fine with a longer delivery period.

We all know of people who get stuck in a particular time frame – they get stuck in the past which they can do nothing about or they focus on being anxious about the future. How many people do we know who waste so much energy stuck in the past, feeling guilty about events long gone or wishing they had acted differently? Or people who spoil the present moment because they are so busy worrying about something that isn't due to happen for weeks ahead? We can conclude that our experience of time is exclusively the result of our mental focus in the moment or in the now, and that can be changed.

Being in the now

The only time is **now**, so consider how you want to experience it. The ability to manage your time will shape your experience of life and your ultimate success. Your experience of time is shaped by your focus. **Stop** for a moment and consider how you are experiencing time right now. Are you enjoying it, wasting it, killing it? You can control your experience by how you focus on time.

Back to the example of a long-distance relationship. The temptation is to focus on the parting that is to follow, even when you've only just been reunited. However, if your focus is instead always in the now, you'll get the maximum enjoyment out of every moment you spend together until the moment that you part, when, of course, you will feel sad. After the goodbyes, you have the choice of either immediately enjoying the next moment of now, or fretting and feeling sad for the rest of the day. This makes a difference to your mood, behaviour and ultimately your results. That's why it is so important to get this message. Too many people waste their lives living in the past or the future.

You can also re-prioritise your life by focusing on what is important as opposed to what is urgent. Have you ever had a day at work when you went home unfulfilled because you spent the whole day on the urgent things as opposed to the important? When you focus on the important you'll find that many of the urgent things just drop off the end of the list. For example, my mother was taken into hospital critically ill one Christmas time. It was actually very liberating to discover that what's important is not the presents or the food or the cards. What's important is for the family all to be together. Nothing else matters – the rest is just a façade. That's when we discovered that we have time now for what is really important – hospital visits – as opposed to spending hours in check-out queues or waiting for a car-parking space. In the office I realised that we were spending most of the day on routine administration matters. I changed our focus – now we focus on what's important, which is getting new customers. Every day we ask ourselves what have we done today to get new business. I also began to set aside time to deal with call-backs and emails. Now the really important things get done without me feeling stressed about them.

Time-saving tricks

Finally, you can save yourself time by finding yourself someone to model. Who has already achieved what you want to achieve? Unless your goal is totally unique someone will have done it already. This will save you enormous amounts of time as you get their years of experience in an instant. For example, read books, listen to CDs, ask people for help. In my experience, if you say to someone that you really admire them and look up to them and that you'd like to learn from them, they are unlikely to turn you down. I have never had anyone turn me down. You can model others by finding out what they believe about themselves and what it is they are doing or their strategies for success, and check out how they use their physiology and how it contributes to their success.

Exercise 21

Enjoying your time

This is a two-week experiment to change your experience of time so stick with it. Each day for the next week keep a diary about how you experience time that day. For example, you might notice that you:

- enjoyed your time
- felt relaxed
- were under time pressures
- did not have enough hours in the day
- felt time flew by
- focused on what is urgent as opposed to important
- or any other experience.

After the first week you will be more familiar with how you currently experience and manage time. During the second week, experiment with changing things. For example:

- focus on what is important rather than urgent
- stop wasting energy 'too late' on the past or worrying 'too early' about the future
- give 100 per cent of your energy in the now
- change your mental focus to having the time you need to get things done.

The power of our emotions

In Chapter 4 we learnt that our results are dependent upon the mood or state we are in at that moment and that our state is driven by how we feel. Our thoughts or internal representations determine how we feel. For example, our result in an interview situation will be determined by how confident we feel in that moment to answer to the best of our ability all the questions we are given. How we feel will be determined by the thoughts we are experiencing. Are we thinking how well we are going to do, or are we terrified of not getting the job?

In NLP we believe it's possible to model ourselves – that we can bring into the 'now' positive states we have experienced from the past. For example, any occasion in the past when we have felt confident we can re-experience in the 'now'. This is an invaluable inner resource that is available any time you are feeling less than resourceful and you need to change your feelings and your state quickly.

We achieve this with a technique called '**anchoring**'. This is a technique to enable you to tap into your inner personal resources when you need them. In particular, anchoring is a way of managing your emotional state. Our ability to choose the best emotional state for a particular situation is one of the most powerful and yet most overlooked and underused skills that we have. We may not be able to control external events and yet we can learn to control the way that we respond to them.

Making anchors work for you

We experience naturally occurring anchors all the time. Remember a time when you walked into a restaurant or even a supermarket when that special piece of music was playing. Maybe it was the song you shared with a special person in your life. In a moment you can be transported back to that place and time and you feel great in the **now**. That is the power of anchors. That is an example of an auditory anchor. We also have visual anchors in our everyday life: we stop (I hope) when we see a red traffic light. The smell of a certain aftershave or perfume provides olfactory anchors; kinaesthetic anchors come from being touched in a certain way. We even experience gustatory anchors when a certain taste transports us back to a special meal. Are you with me so far on this?

In fact, whenever we are experiencing an intense emotional state and something is going on at that moment, such as a piece of music playing, those two things become linked in our minds and they actually get linked neurologically in our brains. The anchor then becomes an unconscious trigger for us. Many relationships fail because of a lack of awareness about negative triggers that are set up over the life of a relationship.

For example, my ex-husband was far less concerned about tidiness than I was. As long as the house was comfortable, he was happy. I, on the other hand, liked the house to be presentable and I got agitated by stuff being left all over the place. We lived in an old barn and our front door opened on to a long dining room; there was no hall. In the dining room was a very long table that could sit 12 people. I was away travelling with my job when the children were small and my ex-husband was a house husband so he looked after everything whilst I was away. Every time I got home from a trip, short or long, I would open the front door and immediately get a sick feeling in my stomach. It was because the table and the floor under the table would be entirely covered over with 'stuff' – papers, letters, clothes and toys. You name it, they were there. Despite our discussing this many times, the outcome was always the same and nothing changed. After a while I began to notice that I dreaded going home and that the sick feeling would occur as I put the key in the door – I didn't even need to see the mess after a while. That is an example of a negative anchor and these take their toll on a relationship.

With NLP we can take positive experiences from the past and use them in the now. While it is wonderful to be able to change your state in the moment, it is even better to be able to consistently feel great and resourceful in those situations that demand your best. When moving towards challenging goals, we need to be able to feel at our best and to know what to do to change our state if we are not in the best of places. We can create resourceful states for ourselves by taking ourselves back to a time when we were resourceful and anchoring that in the now.

The energy button

For the purpose of giving you an experience of programming your body and mind for success, I'm going to take you through a simple exercise to boost your energy and self-confidence. This works in an instant. The more you practise this exercise the more easily you will access that positive state, and you may notice that after a while you only need to think of a time when you were successful and you'll be there because the brain learns very fast. The simple reason is this: the brain consists of millions of neural pathways. Whenever we do something new, we create a new pathway so we can re-access that experience more easily. Each time we repeat a particular behaviour we strengthen the associated neural pathway. I call this the 'energy button exercise'. I call it this because that's the name my children adopted for it as they were growing up. As soon as I learnt about anchoring I taught my children what to do and we set up an 'energy button' for each of them that they could use before exams or at any time when they needed to feel more energised, positive and confident.

Exercise 22

Creating your energy button

Think of specific occasions in the past when you experienced really powerful, positive states. For example, a time when you felt energised, confident, happy, motivated, powerful or successful, fell down laughing or felt totally loved. Remember specific memories, not just general feelings. Work with one memory at a time and repeat this exercise for each memory. The more specific experiences you 'stack' on your energy button the better. And, once you have the button, you can add new experiences as they occur in your life. For example, next time you feel really great, add it to your button.

- Step 1. Let's run through a rehearsal first so you get the idea and the process. Remember a specific time in the past when you felt totally confident. Return to it now in your mind. Imagine floating down into your body and looking through your own eyes. See what you saw, hear what you heard and really feel those feelings of being totally confident.

- Step 2. As you're totally back in the memory, make the colours brighter, the sounds louder and the feelings even stronger.

- Step 3. As you get to the height of the memory and the pictures, sounds and feelings, apply pressure to the knuckle of your first finger on your left hand with the first finger of your right hand.

- Step 4. Continue to apply pressure to the knuckle as you relive the memory through your own eyes.

- Step 5. As the pictures, sounds and feelings begin to ebb away, remove your finger from your knuckle.

- Now you've got the process, repeat steps 1–5 with at least six specific and positive memories. Pick really strong experiences for you. Remember, no one needs to know what they are except you.

- Test: press the knuckle in exactly the same way without accessing a memory and notice how differently you feel. You will feel a combination of all the powerful resourceful states that you stacked – and all without the artificial aids of drugs and alcohol!

Practise this every day. Think about a situation where you want to feel more resourceful and fire off your anchor. Imagine things going perfectly. Next time you have a real-life situation when you need to feel more resourceful, fire off your energy button just before you need it and enjoy the difference. One of my most powerful anchors is when I did the firewalk, the story I used at the beginning of this book. I've added many other experiences to my own energy button over the years. Whenever I need to feel more resourceful, I fire off the button and it works every time. So when people ask me if anchors wear off, I can say absolutely not so long as you use them, and keep adding to them, otherwise we're not giving our brains the opportunity to create the new neural pathways.

Bringing it all together

In this chapter I've focused on three different ways in which you can tap into your own personal resources far more effectively, using energy, time and anchors in a different way to how you may have experienced them in the past. So what if you were to apply these learnings?

I picked these three areas for a specific reason. When we are moving towards the Brilliant Zone and the achievement of our goals, we need to be able to get the most out of our energy – we may need to work long hours at times. We want to feel energised to get done all the things we want to get done. Successful people keep going until they get their goals. We also need to get the most out of time. It's no good focusing on not having enough time to get done all we want to do. We want to use every moment most effectively and to enjoy every moment. Make time work for you, not the other way around.

Don't choose to feel stressed unless there's a very good reason for it. I can tell you that I feel far less stressed than I used to. Does that mean that I work less or have fewer deadlines? Absolutely not!

Finally, being able to control your emotions and change your state in an instant is one of the most valuable lessons I have learnt from NLP. On the rollercoaster of pursuing your goals you need to be able to deal with the rough and the smooth. The smooth is easy to deal with because it's the good news. It's invaluable if you can also take the rough, keep positive, get the learnings and move on as quickly as possible. And, deal with everything in the most resourceful way possible. **Enjoy** getting the most out of yourself, every hour of every day.

Tip: Next time you're feeling pressured, relax and put yourself back into the midst of a positive and happy memory. Count to 10 and start again!

Chapter

9

'When you want to be honoured by others you learn to honour them first.'

Sathya Sai Baba

Influencing with integrity

To really succeed in this world it is important to be able to work with and through others. It's unlikely that you'll achieve your goals entirely by yourself. This chapter is all about how to influence others with integrity using core elements of NLP, such as the presuppositions of NLP, sensory acuity, rapport, communication styles and eye patterns.

The question I get asked more than any other about NLP is whether it is manipulative or not. I often challenge those who pose the question by asking if they know of any sales people who have been taught 'manipulative' techniques. Of course they have. Many tools and techniques have the potential to be used for manipulation – there are many sales people out there with huge sales targets who are taught to sell at all costs, whether the customer needs the goods or not. I would agree that the potential is there in NLP. What makes the difference is how you use the tools you have been taught. That's why this chapter is entitled 'Influencing with integrity'. The difference between manipulation and influence is actually simple. It's all about your intention. If you are focused on a 'win–win' situation, then how can it be manipulation? You achieve your result and so does the other party. Is it manipulation if I use my NLP toolkit to assist my client to achieve the outcome that they want for themselves? With their permission, I'll do whatever it takes to assist them. I see that as my job. Equally, if my goal is to build a successful NLP training company and I sell to people who have told me they need my services – is that manipulation? If I don't make the sale in that situation then somebody else will! Genie Z. Laborde says:

"Once you know how to clarify your own desires (or outcomes) you can use the same techniques to clarify the outcomes of any other party involved in the communication. Achieving that party's outcome while you achieve your own is what I call influencing with integrity."

In contrast, achieving your outcome at the expense of another constitutes manipulation. For example, selling at all costs to achieve your monthly sales target to customers who may or may not want your service is manipulation. For example, I contacted a garage the other day to enquire about a used car that I saw on the internet. The salesman immediately told me that he thought the car was sold. He then came back a few minutes later to tell me the good news... it was still available as the previous sale had fallen through. I observed his strategy with interest and noticed the impact it had on me... he hadn't asked me anything about my requirements at that point and already I was feeling relieved that a car I wasn't sure I even wanted was available!

In contrast, making your sales target by selling to customers who want your service and would gain value from it, is influencing with integrity. That's the difference.

How to build successful relationships

We've already explored a couple of the presuppositions of NLP, such as 'there is no failure only feedback' and 'we have all the resources we need to succeed'. We're now going to explore more of them. When I was studying to become a Practitioner of NLP I found the 'presuppositions' of NLP fundamental to changing the way I relate to others. They frame the context in which the other NLP tools are used. One of the curious things though about the presuppositions is that there is no definitive set published by Bandler and Grinder. They rather emerged as principles that underlie NLP and were made explicit by other NLP developers, such as Robert Dilts. Because of that, you will find variations amongst the literature and this book is no different! According to Toser and Mathison, few of them seem to be original creations of NLP; many came from other fields such as cybernetics. I've selected the ones that I believe have helped me the most in my work with others, and especially in relationship building. These presuppositions succeeded in changing my belief system around the way I communicate and they have the potential to do the same for you. I have also used them with my kids, my family and my team as they are all designed to empower and to give us a greater understanding of and empathy with human behaviour in general. I've re-named them the 'beliefs of world-class communicators' because if you apply them in your daily interactions they will transform your results with others – I guarantee it.

The beliefs of the world-class communicators

Belief	What it means	So what in the context of our goals?
1. Everyone has a different model of the world.	We are all unique.	We learn to accept that everyone is different. This helps us to become more flexible and tolerant of others in the pursuit of our goals.
2. The meaning of your communication is the response you get.	Our communications are only successful if they get us the result that we want.	It puts the responsibility for our communication with us. So, if one approach doesn't work, we need to do something different until we get the outcome we want.

3. There is no failure, only feedback.	We learn from all our experiences.	If we interpret mistakes as failures, we feel defeated. If we interpret mistakes as learning opportunities, we continue to develop and will move faster towards our goals.
4. People do the best they can with the resources they have at the time.	You do the best you can with what you know at that time.	When we act we make the best choice we can with everything we know in that moment. Once we realise this, it allows us to let go of regret and forgive others.
5. The person with the most flexibility will achieve the most.	If you don't get your result first time round, you keep doing something different until you do.	By regularly practising the concepts in this book, you will develop your thinking and your flexibility and achieve your potential.
6. All behaviour has a positive intention behind it.	Why do people do what they do? All behaviour starts with a positive intention by the person doing it. This does not necessarily mean it will also benefit the person or people that the behaviour is 'done to'.	We may not agree with the behaviour, but if we look for the positive intention behind it, this allows us to have more choice in how we respond.

7. We control our minds, and therefore, our results.	We have choices about what we think and we know our thoughts influence our results.	Because results are dependent on our mental state, we want to be in the best state to achieve our goals. We can change our state by changing our thoughts (see back to Chapter 4 for more information).
8. We have all the resources we need to succeed.	People have the capacity to be, do and have whatever they want.	All of us have untapped reserves of qualities, skills and attitudes that we have not yet learned to use (see Chapter 8 for more information). Maximising these will help us achieve our goals faster.
9. Resistance is a sign of a lack of rapport.	When you communicate with another individual or a group, any resistance from them is a sign to you that you need to build better rapport with them.	Rather than blame the other party as 'not interested or bored', use your rapport skills that you will learn in this chapter to get them back on board.
10. There is a solution to every problem.	Finding new solutions to old problems is at the heart of creativity.	This gives us confidence that we will find a way to achieve our goals no matter what challenges we meet on our journey.

11. If something isn't working, do something different.	If you always do what you've always done, you always get what you've always got!	If your strategy isn't working, ask yourself what you can do differently next time. Keep changing your approach until you reach your goal.
12. Anything less than 100 per cent is sabotage.	If you go for something in a half-hearted way, you are stopping yourself from succeeding. Better to do nothing!	Jedi master Yoda in *Star Wars* said: 'Do, or do not. There is no try.' If you want to change your life, then really go for it. If you go for your goals in a half-hearted way, you are likely to sabotage yourself.

Just suppose for a moment that you held these 12 beliefs to be true for you. What difference would they make in your life and to your potential results? I'd like to suggest that you 'trial' them in the context of your journey of change. By trialling them and discovering the ones that have the biggest impact for you, you can, over time, turn them into your own beliefs and thoughts.

Ian – listening for the first time

Ian was in his early fifties and he had wanted to travel for years, however, his wife had a debilitating illness that had prevented it from happening. Sadly, she had died the year before which left a void in Ian's life. He had an opportunity to take early retirement from his civil-service job which he jumped at. He did some personal development work on himself, including a short NLP weekend. He decided to start his travels in a group and he joined a charity trek along the Great Wall of China. He had spent 25 years in the same department and he was the first to admit that he had become rather stuck in his ways. He had been firmly in the Grey Zone. He trained hard for the trek and off he went. At the airport he discovered that he was the oldest by about 20 years. He did his best to communicate with the others but was getting nowhere and felt on the outside. He began to feel that he had made a dreadful mistake and should have stayed with what he knew. He remembered learning about the pre-suppositions of NLP and one in particular played on his mind ... the meaning of the communication is the response you get. Rather than moan about his fellow passengers being on a different planet, Ian decided to experiment with some different approaches. He began to spend time chatting to them about what they liked to do and slowly he began to find some common ground, especially around music. He even discovered the beauty of iPods and bought himself one at the airport on the way home. When he got back he emailed me about this story and how he had almost blown his chance to enjoy his trip. The next time he felt brave enough to travel alone, confident that he could get along with anyone he met.

Now's your chance to experiment with these presuppositions and notice the difference they make to your communication too.

Exercise 23

Act as if ...

For the next four weeks, take each of these and act as if they are true for you. Notice how they begin to reframe your own thoughts and beliefs about your relationships with others. Summarise your learnings below.

My lessons are:

Building your sensory awareness

I was delivering a taster NLP training for a governmental body recently. One of the delegates, a civil servant working in the field of law enforcement, told me about his work. He gets approximately 90 seconds to interview people and decide whether to pass them over to a second line of more intensive enquiry. He has been trained to use his sensory acuity to make these judgements. He starts by asking a series of straightforward questions, such as where the person has travelled from and the route taken and so on. This helps him to 'normalise' or calibrate what's going on in their physiology when they are being truthful. After he has done this, he asks more searching questions and notices if he gets the same non-verbal response or if something has changed. If he gets a different response, it's a possible signal that they are not being truthful and so they get passed onto the assessment team. Although he was sceptical at first, he acknowledges that the techniques are having an impact as the level of interception has increased using these methods. Eye patterns also play a role and we'll find out more about those later in this chapter.

So what if you too were able to learn these powerful tools to improve your own sensory acuity. Of course, you may not have any need to become a human 'lie detector', yet, how useful would it be to notice what's really going on with the people and groups around you? Imagine being a public speaker and noticing and evaluating the state of your audience from moment to moment. Or maybe your goal is to get into a new relationship. How useful would it be to pick up on a potential partner's true feelings towards you? Whatever your situation, these tools are invaluable.

People have naturally occurring levels of sensory acuity. What I mean by this is how we intuitively pick up non-verbal signals in others. You probably know people who are terrible at picking up on these signs, you practically have to hit them over the head for them to notice, whilst others are naturally very good at it. Think about a time when you were going to ask someone a favour but you stopped in your tracks because of some signals you picked up from them. What was it that you noticed that made you stop in your tracks? Often we are unconsciously aware of these signals. What's most important is to start to notice minute changes in others from moment to moment and to work out what that means for our communication with them. Our internal thoughts are expressed through our external behaviour. They literally 'leak' out of our physiology. Remember we learnt earlier that 55 per cent of the impact of our communication is non verbal. However, you also need to learn how to calibrate these changes. For example, if someone you are chatting to suddenly turns bright red in the face you might interpret that as anger. However, that is your mind-read based on your own experiences and perceptions. You will need to check out your interpretation with them. If you were to say to them something like 'are you ok? They might answer saying that they suddenly felt hot whilst you mind-read it as 'anger'. Your mind-read of anger would have been incorrect. That's why a sensory description and then calibration is so important. The alternative is your mind-read and imagination which can be dangerous.

Recognising the non-verbals

What are the kinds of non-verbal reactions to watch out for in others? Some of the changes are easier to spot than others. If you are in peripheral vision, you'll find it easier to spot these changes. This is the vision you naturally use when you are driving. It allows you to take in much more information second by second. When you are driving you need to be aware of what is occurring all around you so you can react quickly if you need to. Sensory acuity is no different. (The opposite of peripheral vision is foveal vision. This is when you focus intently on one thing at a time.)

Things to notice are as follows. Skin colour can change from light to dark or vice versa. The actual tone of the skin might change too. It can go from shiny to not shiny or visa versa. If you're very observant, you may notice the rate or location of breathing changing. It can speed up or slow down or move higher or lower in the body. You can learn a lot from the eyes – the pupil dilation may change or you may notice them defocusing or vice versa. The lips can change too from no lines to lines. However, this is not an exclusive list. Anything else you see also tells you something important!

Milton Erickson was world-class at his levels of sensory awareness. It is alleged that one of his female clients was amazed at his level of skill when Milton saw from the pulse rate at her ankle that her heart rate had decreased.

Exercise 24

Improve your sensory acuity

You'll need someone else to work with you on these exercises. Have fun with them.

True or false

- Explain to your partner that you're going to start by asking them some questions which are true for them. All they need to do is to answer 'yes'.

- Go into peripheral vision.

- Ask your partner some fairly mundane questions, such as 'Is your name (insert their name)?' 'Is today '(insert the name of the day)?' 'Do you live in (insert the name of where they live)?'

- Observe them closely and notice what happens as they tell the truth for each question.

- Then ask them some questions at random. Choose some that are likely to be false for them and ask them to continue answering 'yes' to all your questions.

- Your challenge is watch out for any change in their physiology which will give you some clues that they may not be telling the whole truth.

- See how many 'false answers' you can spot.

Make a note opposite of the physiological changes that you noticed between the true and the false answers.

True:

False:

Congratulations! Were you surprised at how quickly you can begin to sharpen your sensory acuity skills? Excellent sensory acuity is the basis of all world-class communication and the foundation for good rapport. Take time each day to practise your sensory acuity skills. Watch the chat shows on TV. If you have children, notice their responses to your questions. Watch out for those small moment to moment physiological shifts and begin to calibrate what they mean. Your skills will improve quickly if you practise regularly.

What is rapport?

When my readers ask me where all my stories come from for my books I tell them about the key sources that I use. One is the stories of my students as they journey to change their own lives, I also use my own experiences when I feel that others may benefit. In addition, I use my own sensory acuity to observe the behaviour of people. I travel a lot and returning from Turkey recently I had decided to use the four-hour flight to finish this chapter. Imagine my curiosity when I heard an exchange between the cabin crew. The flight was fully booked and several passengers, including a family of four, had missed the flight announcement and were late boarding the plane. They were unable to find four seats together and were blaming everyone except themselves for being late! One crew member turned to the other and said, 'If they had been nicer to me I'd have tried harder to find them seats together.' I smiled as I quickly typed it down word for word, knowing it would appear in this chapter of the book!

You see, good rapport gets things done – it's as simple as that. The family on the plane ended up sitting apart for the entire flight because they missed an opportunity to connect with the air stewardess by building rapport. Genie Z. Laborde described rapport as:

"A somewhat exotic English word derived from the French verb *rapporter*, meaning to bring back or refer. The English meaning – a relation of harmony, conformity, accord, or affinity – indicates the importance of rapport to communication. It is the most important process in any interaction... without rapport you will not get what you want – not money, promotions, not friends.**"**

Rapport is, therefore, a vital tool in helping us to achieve our goals. We learned earlier with the presuppositions, that any resistance in another person towards us is a sign of a lack of rapport. It's our signal that we need to be flexible and do something different with our communication. The key advantages of rapport are that the other person or group will listen to you more readily, feel comfortable in the communication and most importantly are more likely to accept your suggestions to them.

How do you build rapport? Obviously, finding things you have in common, similar behaviours, shared values and beliefs helps enormously. Bandler and Grinder also noticed that there are techniques we can use to build rapport with another person at an unconscious level, i.e. these techniques work outside of their conscious awareness. In NLP we say that when people are 'like' each other, they 'like each other'. If we link this to the fact that non-verbal communication equates to 55 per cent of the impact of communication, we can begin to appreciate that when people are in rapport we notice that their bodies are in a similar position ie they are matching each other's physiology. That's because unconsciously when we feel we are 'like' someone, we are more inclined to 'like' them. For example, if you go into a bar on a Saturday night you can see the people that are unconsciously in rapport as their bodies will be matching. You do not have to hear what they are saying to know this. Equally, if they are out of rapport their bodies will be mismatching each other. That's why when you see a couple arguing they tend to break eye contact and have their bodies away from each other. So we build rapport unconsciously as a natural behaviour. The aim here is to bring it into your awareness and to turn it into more of a conscious behaviour – i.e. you take control of the behaviour and use it with volition.

How do you know that you have rapport? A number of things are likely to happen – you may feel it because you feel at ease with that other person, you may notice a colour shift in yourself or the other person or they might say something like 'I feel like I've known you for ages'.

How do you build rapport?

In NLP the way to build rapport using physiology is by using a technique called matching and mirroring. Matching is when you literally match what the other person is doing, e.g. they cross their left leg over their right leg and you do the same. Mirroring is when you create a mirror image, i.e. they cross their left leg over their right and you cross your right leg over your left. Get it? This means that you use your sensory acuity to observe what they are doing with their physiology and you choose a couple of elements to effectively 'copy'.

Physiology

Here are the elements to watch out for:

● Posture:
  – angle of spine when sitting
  – head to shoulder relationship

- upper body position
- lower body position

- Gestures
- Facial expression and blinking
- Breathing:
  - rate
  - location.

Although it may appear strange and you may worry that the other party will spot what you are doing, don't. Because we build rapport unconsciously all the time, no one will ever notice. Be subtle though. It's over the top to match every part of their physiology. Just pick a few things in the beginning and notice what happens. Facial expressions mean that if you have a customer who uses lots of facial expressions you do the same when you speak. You don't have to match their expressions exactly – do what feels comfortable. It's the same for gestures. If you are communicating with someone who uses a lot of gestures, make sure you add some to your communication when you speak. You will know when you have rapport, because when you change your position they will follow you. This is called 'leading' in NLP. When you have rapport, you will begin to notice how easy it is to get agreement with them.

Exercise 25

Matching body postures

Start to match physiology in many different circumstances – with your partner, friends, children, family members, at work – and notice what happens. If you get into a challenging situation with a family member, start to match and mirror and notice how the disagreement begins to dry up. If you have an important conversation that you need to have with someone, start to match and mirror and notice how you gain agreement more easily. Alternatively, if you want to end a conversation or meeting quickly, start to mismatch physiology and you'll soon get your outcome! Experiment and notice what happens.

Voice tonality

We can also use voice tonality to build rapport. The same principle is used – you match voice tonality, and, as tonality accounts for 38 per cent of the impact of communication, this also has a major impact.

How do you do it? If you really tune into a person's voice, you'll begin to notice that some voices are high or low, loud or soft and tempo is fast or slow. Really tune into the 'song' of the voice. For example, the pitch of a voice tends to go up and down as a person speaks. Notice when their voice goes higher and when it goes lower. For example, is it a voice that goes 'up' at the end of most sentences? To match tonality you use the same features in your voice. You do not have to match the voice exactly; just enough for the other person to feel a sense of familiarity. Don't match accents – that is a recipe for disaster. And, if you are a male matching a female or vice versa, please do not try to match the other person as it will sound very odd! Just take your voice up a notch if you are a man and down a notch if you are a woman. Start to use your sensory acuity to begin to notice the differences in tonality.

People often ask me what to do when someone is shouting at you. In this situation, you should raise your tone, i.e. move closer to theirs and use the same words you would have used normally. In the past, customer-services staff were taught to be quiet and encourage the person to quieten down when angry. However, in NLP, we feel this has the impact of mismatching and is even more likely to add 'fuel to the fire'. This is, of course, also the technique to use to build rapport over the telephone.

Exercise 26

Matching voice tonality

Start to match voice tempo first. Notice different rates of speech. Later move onto matching tones. If you get into a challenging situation, start to match tempo and tone and notice how quickly the disagreement begins to dry up. Experiment often with this to build your flexibility. Notice what happens.

Words

Finally, let's discover how to match words. There are a number of things to listen out for. We're going to re-visit our communication styles that we discovered in Chapter 5 and learn how to match the different styles that people use. In addition, listen out for any key words that person uses over and over again. Start to use them in your own language. For example, if someone uses the word 'absolutely' a lot, start to use it when you are speaking to them. Also, listen out for common experiences, interests and values that you share and bring them into the conversation. Don't pretend though – there's too high a risk that you'll come unstuck! Also, notice the content chunks that they use, i.e. do they use short or long sentences? Modify your content chunks to match theirs.

Learning to speak a new language

Please go back to Exercise 11. Which communication styles were your most and least preferred? Do you notice that you often use the literal words of your style? For example, what style of person would use the word 'feel' in their language? The really clever thing is that you can begin to spot other people's communication styles from the words or predicates that they use. Appendix 2 lists examples of the types of words and phrases each style will primarily use. These words reflect whether they are thinking using their *visual, auditory, kinesthetic* or *audio digital* systems, and this gives you an insight into how their brain is sorting information at the time. You can't tell what a person is thinking but you can have a good idea how they are thinking! For example, visual people will use words like 'see, clear, illuminate,' etc. and phrases like 'I can see that'. They are literally telling you that they are making a picture in their minds. A kinaesthetic person will use words like 'feel, touch, grasp' and phrases like 'that feels good to me'. An auditory person will use words like 'hear, listen sounds' and phrases like 'that sounds good to me'. An audio digital person will use words like 'sense, think, experience' and phrases like 'that makes sense to me'.

By listening to the words someone uses, you can begin to identify their preferred style. This, added to spotting the characteristics we discussed earlier in Chapter 5, will make it very easy to identify the style of the person you are communicating with. It's that simple – listen for the words which indicate in what sense the person is thinking, and adjust your communication style to match. Much miscommunication comes from people mismatching the style of the other person. That breaks rapport. Using the same language will build rapport very quickly. For example, if you keep using auditory words to a visual person, they will unconsciously have to translate internally to their own system. This takes time, can be difficult for some people, and does not build rapport. You will find that you get along naturally more easily with those people who have the same preference as you. If you have a challenge in some of your relationships, you may have been unknowingly breaking rapport until now!

Exercise 27

Speaking a new language

Start off by picking a significant person in your life and listen to the types of words they use. You will notice they will probably use all types of the visual, auditory and kinaesthetic words... but one type will usually predominate. Observe their physical characteristics too. What do they tell you about their most likely preferred style? When you add their words together with their physiology you have a very powerful tool for building rapport. Practise translating your language to match their preferred style. You may find that translating into a language that is your least preferred style is the biggest stretch for you. That means it's the one you need to practise most. The great thing is that it doesn't matter if you get it wrong as you're no worse off than when you didn't know about this stuff! You can then use your sensory acuity to notice when they begin to lose interest... that's a sure sign you need to pick another style and experiment with that. You'll know when you have their attention as they will be really engaged in what you have to say.

For example:

If they say 'I don't see your point', don't say, 'Let me help you understand'. Say instead: 'Let me show you what I mean.'

If they say, 'What you're suggesting doesn't feel right to me', don't say, 'I think it makes perfect sense'. Say instead: 'Let's get a handle on the points in another way.'

If they say 'I've stopped listening to you', don't say, 'You're insensitive'. Say instead: 'Let's talk it through.'

Then practise with those around you, and listen to conversations on radio or television to develop your skills. Before long, you will find yourself doing it automatically.

Jamie and Julie – practice makes perfect

Jamie had recently moved in with his girlfriend and was struggling with the way they were communicating. It felt like they were speaking different languages at times. So much for the language of love! A typical argument was about the state of their house. It would go something like this:

JAMIE: I can't see what all the fuss is about. I've only asked you to keep the house clean and tidy.

JULIE: That's right, it's obvious you're feeling bad about it but for me the house doesn't feel comfortable when it's tidy. Why are you so pushy about it all the time? I didn't grasp that living together would be like this.

After Jamie learned about different communication styles it was like a light bulb coming on. He realised that his preference was a visual one and Julie's was a kinaesthetic one. He started to translate her language like this:

I really want to get in touch with how you feel about this. Please help me get a handle on it. How can we find a solution that we both feel great about?

Once Jamie had better rapport with Julie, he could find ways of expressing himself that she empathised with. Their relationship rapidly improved and got even better when Jamie shared what he knew with Julie so she could use more visual language to match his.

We have now learned how to build rapport using physiology, tonality and words. Now it's time to start practising. By practising consciously, you'll soon find that you begin to do things unconsciously. You may be surprised to notice how much you've learned and are already using. These skills are available to improve all the key relationships in your life.

NLP eye patterns

In the weeks following the discovery of representational systems (or communication styles, as I've called them), Bandler and Grinder discovered something else that was quite extraordinary. They discovered that there was a specific eye movement linked to each of the different communication styles. There are few patterns of NLP that can be claimed to be totally original (as opposed to modelling of world-class behaviour), the discovery of eye movements is one such pattern. Grinder describes how they were 'astonished by the regularity and obviousness of the associated eye patterns'. They coded their independent observations into what has now become known as the NLP 'funny face'.

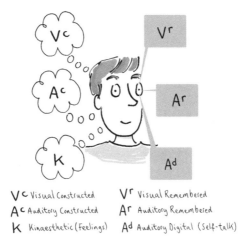

V^c Visual Constructed   V^r Visual Remembered
A^c Auditory Constructed   A^r Auditory Remembered
K Kinaesthetic (Feelings)   A^d Auditory Digital (Self-talk)

These are the eye patterns of a 'normally' organised person as you look at them. They are independent of language and culture. Occasionally, people are reverse organised, i.e. their patterns are a mirror image of those shown above. Here's how it works. When you:

- look up and to your left, you are remembering an image of something from the past, e.g. your favourite holiday as a child;

- look up and to your right, you are imagining or constructing an image of something, e.g. imagining what you would look like in that new suit/dress;

- look across and to your left, you are remembering a sound from the past, e.g. your favourite track;

- look across and to your right, you are constructing a sound, e.g. hearing you singing your favourite track;

- look down and to your left, you are talking to yourself or working out a logical calculation or generating a set of logical criteria;

- look down and to your right, you are into your feelings, e.g. you are feeling happy about something.

Exercise 28

Seeing magic

Here is a set of questions that will help you to spot the eye patterns of another person. You'll need a volunteer for this exercise. Ask each question and watch where the eyes of your partner go. You will need to be fast so make sure you memorise the question and then ask it as you are looking at your partner – otherwise you'll miss the action! Also, change the images if they don't mean anything to your partner, e.g. change Darth Vader to something meaningful to your partner if they don't watch *Star Wars*, etc.

Eye pattern elicitation questions (used with permission. © The Tad James Co, Tad and Adriana James). Remember this is as you look at the person.

1. **Visual remembered (looking up to their left)**

   a. What was the colour of the room you grew up in?

   b. What was the colour of your front door when you were a kid?

2. **Visual construct (looking up to their right)**

   a. What would your room look like if it were painted green with purple spots?

   b. What would your car look like with a Rolls-Royce radiator grill and turbo go-faster stripe?

3. **Auditory remembered (looking across to their left)**

   a. What was the last thing I said to you?

   b. Can you hear your favourite piece of music all of the time?

4. **Auditory construct (looking across to their right)**

   a. What would I sound like with Darth Vader's voice?

   b. What would your favourite piece of music sound like played backwards?

5. **Auditory digital (looking down to their left)**

   a. What was the first thing you said to yourself this morning?

   b. Can you recite your national anthem to yourself?

6. **Kinaesthetic (looking down to their right)**

   a. What does it feel like to stand barefoot on a wet carpet?

   b. What does it feel like to put on a shirt or blouse?

You may find some odd things happening that you didn't expect. For example, you might ask a 'kinaesthetic' question and notice that the person goes into visual remembered first before they go into their kinaesthetic eye pattern. This is often because many people have a lead system as well as a preferred communication style or representational system. For example, if you ask me how I feel about my partner, and I have a visual lead, I may see a picture of them in my head (visual remembered) before going into my kinaesthetics or feelings. You can ask your partner what they are doing on the inside if they don't do exactly what you were expecting. Once you bring it to their conscious awareness, they will tell you something like: 'I see a picture of my partner first and then I get a feeling'. It's often the case, but not always, that your preferred communication style or representational system is the same as your lead system. If you remember back to my civil-servant delegate, he also uses eye patterns to reinforce his assessments. For example, after he has normalised answers he may ask the same question again. If he notices the person using a visual construct eye pattern, he knows that they are likely to be 'making up' the answer this time and it's another cue to pass them over to the second line assessment team.

Pulling it all together

Using eye patterns, you can literally 'see' what people are doing inside their heads from moment to moment. Just imagine how powerful it would be if you saw the person you were communicating with move their eyes into kinaesthetic and you were able to match with your language at that moment. You could say 'How do you feel about that...?'. As if by magic you would build exquisite rapport with them there and then. If you add this to your techniques for sensory acuity and rapport building, you have a powerful toolkit to influence those around you in the moment. They will be amazed at how you appear to be able to 'read' their minds. They will feel comfortable because you appear to be like them and they will be much more likely to accept your suggestions and recommendations because you have rapport.

Remember, too, that you should always use these tools with integrity and a positive intention to assist those around you to make decisions that you know will be useful to them. That way it's a 'win–win' scenario for both of you. By doing this you'll find it becomes far easier to achieve your goals too. These tools enable us to be far more flexible in the moment and we know from the presuppositions of NLP that the person with the most flexibility will achieve the most. Any resistance comes from a lack of rapport which is then your signal to be flexible enough to experiment with something different, such as matching physiology, tonality, language or noticing eye patterns. It's a powerful toolkit for improving communication so use it wisely!

Tip: We all influence and how we choose to influence is in our hands.

Chapter

10

'People are responsible for their own performance.
There's feedback all around you – if you pay attention.
If you're not getting enough feedback, ask for it.'

Gina Imperato

Step up with feedback

'Can I give you some feedback?'

How many of us have experienced that uncomfortable feeling in the pit of our stomachs at the mere mention of the word 'feedback' or 'appraisal' or even 'performance review meeting'? Be honest with yourself. If you had the choice of getting some feedback or cleaning your bathroom, which would you choose? Few of us enjoy hearing about our shortcomings and even fewer people enjoy describing others' shortcomings to them – although some of you may have had bosses in the past who seemed to relish hoarding up all your feedback to a once-a-year event that left you reeling and still trying to remember most of the examples given as they happened so long ago.

My goal in this chapter is to assist you to come to understand feedback as a gift – a gift that will catapult you to the next level of performance. Feedback is how we know whether what we are doing is working. It's how we know whether we are on track. If we don't know how we are doing, we run the risk of investing time, energy and money into ineffective strategies – like the hamster running around in the hamster wheel. If it's not working, we are in danger of just doing more of it unless we get feedback. We live in a world of instant feedback as far as email and text messages are concerned, yet few of us thrive on getting instant personal performance feedback. In fact, most of us have strategies for doing just the opposite, to keep personal performance feedback at bay with well-developed avoidance strategies and smoke screens.

I once witnessed a moment on a course when two best friends were asked to give each other feedback. One of the two told me that she felt very awkward about doing this. I was very curious at this point as I knew how long they had been friends. I asked her if she had ever given her friend feedback about anything that really mattered in the whole of their twenty-year friendship. She never had. I asked her what she would say to her friend if she were to give her the feedback. She said that she would suggest to her that she wore more brightly coloured clothes, as she always wore dark clothes that didn't suit her. I then asked what had prevented her from giving her friend that feedback for over 20 years. She said that she didn't want to hurt her feelings. I reframed the scenario for her by asking whether she thought it was better for her friend to always stay the same or to have the opportunity to do something different and potentially feel better about herself. She looked at me and said that she'd never thought of it like that – that she could have held her friend back. She went back to the group, took a deep breath and gave her friend the feedback. It wasn't as scary as either of them had anticipated and it allowed them to be truly honest with each other for the first time in 20 years.

Feedback in the moment helps us to get to the next level **faster** because it helps us to adjust our actions in real time rather than at some arbitrary measurement point or, even worse, never find out. All good businesses actively seek feedback in order to find out what they are doing right for their customers, and what needs to change.

Feedback is also a key coaching tool in terms of personal development. It is the main contribution that I can make with the individuals and companies with whom I work. If they were better and more willing to give each other feedback, then my role would soon become redundant.

What is feedback?

Feedback is about evaluation; it is not only about what needs to be improved but also what was good about the performance. That second part can often be missed in our society which seems too focused on feedback in terms of criticism – no wonder it is feared by most. Feedback only works if it leads to a change. If the recipient listens to the feedback and integrates it then it has achieved its purpose. In our society the fear of being honest often leads to the 'halo' effect. The halo effect is when we give over-complimentary feedback because we do not want to hurt the feelings of the recipient or we do not want to rock the boat. I often term this as 'bullshit feedback'! Often whole organisations collude with this system because it keeps everything running smoothly. I've known old friends giving each other top marks on annual appraisal forms which had nothing to do with their performance.

Why do we behave in this way? Management expert, Jerry B. Harvey, argues that we are tempted to say nothing or dress up negative feedback because of the following:

- Action anxiety – giving honest feedback creates intense anxiety in the giver as they think about acting in accordance with what they know to be right. As a result, they act in a manner incongruent with their beliefs.

- Negative fantasies – the giver builds up in their minds the negative consequences of speaking the truth until they are completely paralysed by the thought of it.

- Fear of separation – probably the biggest reason for 'bullshit feedback' as the giver fears separation from the norm or the group if they take the risk of speaking out. If we think back to our two friends, one was terrified of her feedback changing the relationship she had and losing the friendship she valued.

This gives us the reasons why 'bullshit feedback' is so prevalent in our society. NLP assists us to change our view about feedback – both the delivery of it and the receipt. We know that the presupposition of NLP is that:

There is no failure only feedback.

In other words, there is only learning. If you truly believe this, you will seek the learning that comes from all experiences in order to develop yourself. Feedback then becomes something to be welcomed and not something to be feared. Feedback is then fundamental to your development.

There are other beliefs that also support our ability to give and receive feedback.

Everyone's perception is their own truth

We may not agree with the feedback we have been given but it's true for the giver in that situation. Each person's perception is unique to them and represents their own model of the world. That does not make it right or wrong, it is just true for them. By accepting the feedback from someone, we are accepting that part of ourselves as they experience it. If everyone in a group gives an individual the same feedback, then there is something for them to think about.

"If you can spot it, you got it."

I heard NLP trainer, Sue Knight, say this at the NLP annual conference. In other words, what we recognise in others is true about ourselves. The characteristics in others that touch us emotionally are a pointer towards those things being characteristics that we don't like in ourselves. You may notice that you dissociate from the characteristics that you don't like in others. Yet, these are often 'blind spots' in us. To see something in others, we have to have that 'structure' in our thinking too, otherwise we would not recognise it. For example, I recently gave feedback to my daughter about not paying her monthly housekeeping allowance on time and then recognised that behaviour in myself when paying business bills! That was an example of a 'blind spot' for me.

Taking on these beliefs helps us to begin to change our own mindset around feedback and to begin to see it as something precious. It also starts to become clear that feedback is all around us if we take the time to seek it out. It's not just about what others tell us, we get feedback from everything we do. For example, if everybody stays quiet when you suggest something, the chances are that their silent feedback means they don't like the idea.

How to give and receive feedback

In NLP, a popular approach for giving feedback is the 'feedback sandwich'. It isn't the only approach but it's one that I personally find very useful. All change happens at an unconscious level and the unconscious mind needs to hear feedback quickly after the event. Feedback that is stored up during the year for the day of the performance appraisal meeting is a waste of time. One of the most common complaints about feedback is that it takes place too long after the event being reviewed occurred. Fast feedback is built into the daily routine, ideally at the moment that the event happens, or at the end of a meeting, or at the end of the day.

What specifically did they do well?

What can they do better next time?

What did they do well overall?

The feedback sandwich process is made up of three stages, while maintaining eye contact at all times. First, check that you are in rapport with the person and then tell them what they did well – that gets the unconscious mind open and interested in listening. Next, you give the person specific suggestions as to what they can do even better next time – this is often called the 'meat' in the sandwich. Finally, you end with an overall positive statement. You can also confirm the learning by asking the person receiving the feedback what they will do differently next time. The important thing is to say the feedback the way it is. Be as direct as possible – do not leave the opportunity for misinterpretation, and give as many specific examples as you can. Vague feedback is meaningless.

The unconscious mind hears the initial positive statement which makes it much more receptive to hearing the areas for improvement. Again, it's important to focus on what the person should do differently and not on what they shouldn't do. As we learnt earlier, the unconscious mind cannot process a negative. Remember 'Don't think of a blue tree'? To not think of a blue tree you have first to think of a blue tree. So if we focus on what we shouldn't do, we attract that exact thing to us.

Steve – experiencing the importance of the feedback sandwich

Steve is known as 'Meat Man', meaning that he gives very direct feedback in the middle of the sandwich. He tells a story of when his boss used the feedback sandwich with the team. Steve had spent years in the army and did not consider that he needed to hear the good stuff – he just wanted the meat. He told his boss that he could be straight with him. His boss asked him three times if that was what he truly wanted and he said 'yes'. The boss then began to give him just the meat. Several weeks went by and he realised that he was avoiding his boss. In fact, if he heard him coming along the corridor, he would slip into another office to hide away. He couldn't understand his behaviour until one day the penny dropped. Receiving the feedback was nothing about being 'tough' and it was all about balance. If you give compliments, you will receive compliments and that helps to build confidence. He asked his boss to return to the feedback sandwich and he soon began to notice that he was much happier to bump into him in the corridor again.

Receiving feedback is a fundamental precursor to being able to and having the right to give it. Your ability to receive feedback is central to continuous learning and growth as well as being key to healthy relationships both in business and in life. Receiving feedback is also a skill to be learnt and practised. To receive feedback you need to hold the beliefs discussed above in your mind. If you see everything as feedback then the potential of failure does not exist. That makes it easier to listen to and consider the feedback you are given. Before you receive feedback get yourself into a resourceful state. Remember how we learnt to anchor a positive state from the past (see Chapter 8). The best states may be openness, humility, self-confidence or curiosity. Always anticipate feedback and always invite it when appropriate so that feedback is in constant supply to you.

The specific skills for receiving feedback are as follows:

- Listen carefully and keep an open mind. You cannot make judgements on the validity if you have a closed mind.

- Suspend judgement. Do not put up your defences; rather take your time and make some mental notes to check out later.

- Let the giver finish. Wait until they have got to the end and you have a full picture.

- Paraphrase to check out what you have heard and to clarify your perception.

- Ask for specific examples if they are not given.

- Avoid arguing, denying, justifying or minimising. It's their point of view. Decide what you want to do with the information. Look for patterns with other feedback you have received before.

- Respond in a way that presupposes acceptance, saying things like 'In what ways do I do this?' and 'What effect does this have on you?'.

- Gather information from other sources.

- Decide what you want to do next. Think about how you can use the information to improve your results. Imagine yourself having taken on board the feedback and now behaving in a way that demonstrates you have done so.

- Thank the person for giving you feedback.

The ultimate measure of the success of either giving or receiving feedback is that you or the other person integrates the learning from it.

Rachel – taking a risk to develop an amazing relationship

Rachel and Eddie had been together for five years and their relationship was on the rocks. They had little in common and spent the majority of their spare time with their friends. Rachel learnt about feedback on one of our programmes and decided to use it as a last-ditch attempt to save her marriage as she still loved her husband. They did a deal with each other that they would both put 100 per cent commitment into understanding each other's needs for the first time in their relationship. This involved them being totally honest with each other about their feelings and about what was good and what needed to change in their relationship. It took courage to give the level of feedback both ways that was required. Yet, in those most open moments they learnt more about each other and what made them both happy than ever before. They agreed to focus on meeting each other's needs in an atmosphere of deep-felt understanding. Their relationship moved to an entirely new level as they saw each other for the first time and enjoyed developing and changing as their levels of understanding grew.

Exercise 29

Practising giving and receiving feedback for yourself

Part 1 – giving feedback

Go through the questions and decide who you want to give feedback to and for what purpose. This will allow you to plan for the event. Remember to consider what it felt like to give the feedback as well.

● The person I want to give feedback to is:

- This is what I want to say and the outcome I want to achieve by giving this feedback:

- Record below what it felt like to give the feedback.

Part 2 – receiving feedback

This time, identify three people who are significant to you in the context of the area about which you want the feedback, e.g. business, career, health and fitness, etc. Pick one person you like, one person you admire and one person who you have difficulties with.

- The people I want feedback from are:
  1.

  2.

  3.

- Ask them for feedback using the feedback sandwich. Follow the guidelines set in this chapter for you to receive the feedback in the most resourceful and effective way.

- Record below what you learned from the process.

What if you were to integrate feedback in your everyday life?

Incorporating feedback will help you to fast-track your development process. In terms of your goals, if you were to get feedback on your actions, you will eventually find a way through. I guarantee you that. You will notice that your relationships with people in all areas of your life will improve. They will become deeper and more meaningful as congruence, openness and honesty become the focus instead of avoidance. Some relationships may feel uncomfortable and this is because not enough rapport has been built at the start of the process. If you find that some of your colleagues, friends and family do not want to play the feedback game then consider the long-term value of these relationships – at best they can only be described as shallow. Most importantly, you will become even better at what you do and your ability both to give and receive feedback will be noticed and admired.

Tip: Giving feedback once a year is like dieting only on your birthday and wondering why you're not losing weight.

Chapter **11**

'A journey of 1,000 miles begins with a single step.'

Lao-tzu, Chinese philosopher

Get started

Your moment of truth

You have the power to control what you think, you have the power to control how you feel and you have the power to control what you do. Now it is your **moment of truth** because it's time to take action. You decided that you want more from your life. You've worked on your goals and I've assisted you with the mindset and beliefs you need for success. Now it's your time to go for it. Some of you may be starting to feel a little unresourceful as we get down to your personal moment of truth and that's normal. Recognise where you are and where those feelings are coming from. If you need to work more on your mindset, then do it **now** because we're about to rock and roll!

And, I have to let you into a secret that successful people already know – one of the biggest myths is that it takes a superhuman act to achieve our goals. It's just not the case. It's the small decisions that we make that affect our destiny as much as the big ones. If we make enough small decisions then we will get there. I once asked my teacher:

'What's the secret of achieving your goals?'

I still think about his answer at least once a day. He said:

'Keep going until you do!'

It is a remarkably simple and very wise statement that has guided me through big life challenges. Stick with it and you will always achieve your goal. Last Christmas, there was a joke that one of my children read out of their cracker at the dinner table. It said:

'How do you eat an elephant?'

The answer was:

'In small chunks.'

It's the same for your goals. Each time we make a decision we begin to create our future in advance and each time we take a decision there are consequences. It's important to think these through and know that you cannot plan for every eventuality. It's impossible. You have to jump off the edge of the cliff, have faith and learn as you fly.

❝I have long since come to believe that people never mean half of what they say, and that it is best to disregard their talk and judge only their actions.**❞**
                                                            Dorothy Day

When I set up my business I had read all the management books, and I had done my NLP training that taught me if you are willing to do whatever it takes to achieve your goals you will get there. I had complete belief that my business would be a success because I believed myself to be good at what I do as a trainer, consultant and coach. I believed that I would be able to grow a successful company on these competencies. I'd planned everything that I could think of – website, brochures, networking, offices and venues.

So, when I had to postpone my first course I was bitterly disappointed. Why? Because I soon discovered that not only did I need to be a world-class trainer and coach, I also needed to know how to grow a business and be a successful businesswoman. Whilst I was great at training, I was rubbish at marketing, sales and financial management. All important qualities when you run a business. That came as a shock to me and I had to buy in or develop these competencies very fast. I decided that I would get part-time assistance to set up and run my financial systems and marketing and I knew that I needed to get much better at selling myself. So I began to find great sales-people and successful entrepreneurs to model. The important thing was that I was taking action – sometimes that felt like two steps forward and one step back, but it doesn't matter *as long as you are moving ahead.*

Our society is so used to instant gratification through the web, emails, text messages and TV. Yet, we need to have a long-term focus if we are really to succeed. For example, if I had taken a short-term view after I postponed my first training programme, The Change Corporation may have ceased to exist there and then. Take small, simple steps and when things don't go to plan get the learnings and work out what you need to do differently next time.

If you take no action, then simply nothing will change. I'm reminded of a trip to MFI that I made two years ago because I wanted some new bookshelves for my study at home. I'd seen the ones I wanted and was delighted because after Christmas they were in the sale. I bought two small bookshelves and dis-covered when I went to pay that they needed to be put together at home. In other words, they were flat-packed. I was rather disappointed to find that out and, of course, that explained why they were cheaper than some of the other styles. Anyway, I didn't have much cash flow at the time so I bought them and proceeded to take them home in the back of my car. Even haul-ing the two large boxes in and out was a real effort. I put these boxes in the back of my garage where they were out of the way. Two years on I hadn't even opened the boxes and in the end I took them to a car-boot sale and sold them to a DIY enthusiast.

That's what it's like if you take no action after reading this book. It's like having all the secrets to success in a flat-packed furniture box waiting for the day you will have the motiva-tion to get started. And, the longer you leave it, the less likely it is that you will take the action you need to take. We learnt earlier about German physicist and Nobel Laureate, Werner Heisenberg, who proposed in 1927 that 100 per cent certainty does not exist. Therefore, if you wait for 100 per cent cer-tainty before you take any action, you will never move forward. Successful people know they will never know everything and they go for it anyway. That's been my saving grace in many tight situations, that and 'acting as if'.

I've come across a number of people who expected me to sprinkle 'magic dust' on them so they would leave the room having been 'changed'. I wish it were that easy. If I had 'magic dust', then I would be a very rich woman by now. A person or book can only be your tour guide – you have to take responsibility for making the changes you want in your life.

So, if you are hoping for some fairy dust then you are reading the wrong book. It's time for you to work out what your first step is to be, and to get started – because nothing changes until you take that first step.

How to get started

"Do or do not. There is no try."   Jedi Master Yoda

When getting started, the most important thing to remember is to go for your goals at a 100 per cent level of commitment. I love this quote from *Star Wars* because trying to take action is like taking no action at all. If I were to say to you that I will 'try' to meet you for lunch next week, do you think I'm really committed to meeting you? I don't think so. The word 'try' is used in the English language as an excuse for doing something in a half-hearted way or not doing it at all. Related to this, we've already come across in Chapter 9 the NLP presupposition:

Anything less than 100 per cent is sabotage.

That means if you are not prepared to go for something at 100 per cent then don't waste your time and money because you will be sabotaging your results from the start. For example, when I stood at the foot of the fire on the first night of my fire-walking trainer's training I did not 'try' to walk the fire. That would be asking for an injury. I focused 100 per cent commitment throughout my mind and my body to walking the fire and I walked safely that night and every other night.

Lily and Tony – sabotaging their lifestyle

My clients bought a new house that needed complete renovation. They were newly married and both of them had been keen to take on the project. They both also had busy and demanding jobs. Months went by and they felt like they were living in the middle of a building site with neither of them having the time to deal with the house situation. This put pressure on their relationship and they were close to a trial separation when they came to see me. They began to understand that the house renovation had been too ambitious a project for them at that stage of their lives when they needed to be focused on other things. They were more passionate about their careers and having fun together. They sold the house, bought a brand new property and got their lives back, knowing that they would take on a renovation project when they could give it the attention it deserved.

To get started there are a number of steps that you need to take. Here is a summary from what we've covered so far.

● Firstly, apply the techniques in this book – set goals, focus on what you want, operate at cause, learn to believe in yourself, use your internal resources to the full. If you ever begin to feel unresourceful when you consider taking action ask yourself, 'For what purpose do I feel like this? Is it a limiting belief I still need to change?' Start to create new reference points for yourself.

● Secondly, be willing to be flexible in your approach and be prepared to do something different – not, as I've said before, what you've always done. Ask yourself whether you are prepared to change your circumstances to get your goal. Are you prepared to set boundaries and stick to them? For example, if there's something you want to change in your relationship, are you prepared to set a new boundary and stick to it? I have a client who has taken back her boyfriend more times than I can count because when it comes to her moment of truth she will not enforce the boundary and do something different. I'm wondering when the pain will become great enough that she finally does something different.

- Thirdly, and very importantly, be prepared to do **whatever it takes** to reach your goal. When I ask at my taster sessions whether people are prepared to do whatever it takes, I can guarantee that a few will always put their hands up immediately. Some will look around first to see who else has put their hands up and others go into fear mode because they do not know what that might mean for them.

Fear is like many other things – we can build it out of all proportion in our heads. The fear feels worse because we focus on it as opposed to focusing on all the things that are going well. My strategy when working on fear is to ask myself and my clients, 'What is the worst thing that could happen to you on your path to achieving your goal?' In my experience, I've found that once you have come to terms with the 'worst thing', it very rarely happens. Also, as you have already seen, taking small baby steps towards your goal can be a great way of overcoming any fear you used to have.

Are you ready to get started?

Developing your own 'personal journey plan'

We are going to work through an exercise that will take you on the journey. I have run four marathons in my life so far. I always think that a marathon starts and finishes with a single step and that every step I run is a step nearer to the finish line. It makes the journey easier and motivates me to keep going even when the road seems very long.

When we worked on our goals, we worked backwards from the point at which we had achieved our goal. This time, as we put our personal journey plans together, we are going to work outwards from now. We are going to focus on the next year to keep the plans manageable. Each year in December I go through a process to revisit what I've achieved the year before and to review my goals for the following year. Some of these goals will stand alone; others will support your longer-term goal. The important lesson is to keep the momentum going.

Go back to the goals you set for yourself in Chapter 3. Consider for a moment the goals you set for yourself at one month, three months, six months and one year. Begin the exercise by putting the date one year from today's date and write down again all the goals you set for yourself for the next year. As you write them down, begin to think about what actions you need to take to achieve each of these goals:

- within 24 hours
- within 48 hours
- within one week
- within one month
- within three months
- within six months.

Get the idea? When you break the goal and actions into smaller chunks it's easy to get started. The other invaluable learning that I have got from this exercise is to find yourself a journey plan buddy. Seriously, this should be someone who you respect and who will give you a hard time should you not stick to your commitments. Your buddy, therefore, shouldn't necessarily be your best friend who will commiserate with all your excuses; they should be someone who will challenge you and remind you of what it is you are going for. Ideally, it should be someone you know who is also reading this book, or else someone who will be open and honest with you and who will give you a hard time if necessary. If there is no one that you can think of worthy of the role, then email me (details at the back of the book) because we keep a buddy register and will put you in touch with someone who can help you and who will ask the same in return from you. Book appointments with your buddy at one week, one month, three months, six months and at the one-year anniversary of this plan. This can be in person, by phone or by email. You should give your buddy a copy of your goals and your plan.

Exercise 30

My personal journey plan

1. What will I have achieved by (date in one year's time)?

   - ....
   ....

   - ....
   ....

   - ....
   ....

   - ....
   ....

   - ....
   ....

   - ....

2. What's the first step I need to take in the next 24 hours?

3. Forty-eight hours?

4. One week?

5. One month?

6. Three months?

7. Six months?

8. One year?

Remember to send a copy of your first year's action plan to your buddy and repeat this process each year until you achieve your goal.

What if you take action now?

As soon as you start to take action, you begin to create your future in the now. Your goal will feel more and more real as you move ahead. Tell people who you know will support you as you pursue your goal. Write your goal down and stick it all over your house and your office. A friend of mine wanted to replace her fireplace in her lounge. She had bought a new house but the fireplace was brick built and old fashioned. She saw the picture of the fireplace she wanted in a home design magazine but it was hugely expensive as it had won many design awards. However, she fell in love with it and cut out the photograph. She stuck the photograph on the front of her fridge and every day she looked at it. One year later she was looking at the real thing in her living room.

You know that every step you take is a step closer to your goal. Things will change around you. You will notice that you begin to attract the people and opportunities that will help you the most. As we have discussed, it doesn't matter whether you know exactly how you are going to achieve your goal. Stay focused on it, be open to possibilities and be ready to take action. Some people assume that they have to take enormous steps. That isn't true. The biggest secret of all is to keep going and to be prepared to do something different until you get there.

Tip: Whatever happens, stay in the ring. As Winston Churchill said, 'Never give in. Never give in. Never, never – in nothing, great or small, large or petty – never give in, except to convictions of honour and good sense. Never yield to force. Never yield to the apparently overwhelming might of the enemy.'

Chapter

12

'Always bear in mind that your own resolution to
succeed is more important than any one thing.'

Abraham Lincoln

Do you want it or what?

We've come a long way together, haven't we? So don't blame me if as a result of reading this book you become successful. My goal has been to inspire you to think and feel differently about your life. To see what is possible and to go for what you want in your world.

Throughout this book I have given you ideas, skills, tools and the motivation to change your life, to really go for what you want. Now, as you are nearing the end of this book, you have a choice to make. You can be happy that you have learned something new and slip quietly back into the Grey Zone. Or you can move to the 'C side' and begin to nurture those powerful beliefs that will create what you want. If so, you are ready to take the first step. Perhaps you have already taken it in your mind or in reality as you made your way through all the transformational exercises in this book. Change leads to more change. Every step you take brings a success that will inspire you to make the next move. You've learned that the most important thing is to keep going until you reach your goal.

To achieve your goal is an amazing experience and I wish you many of them.

How do you want to be remembered?

So the question is, what do you want your legacy to be? It doesn't matter where you are right now or how old you are. It is never too late to change. I wish for you to live your life fully. Live your life in the now. Give everything you do your 100 per cent commitment. Experience everything that you get the opportunity to. If someone asks you to get involved in something, just say 'yes'. That's another one of my philosophies of life. And the more fearful you are of the opportunity the better, as the learning will be greater. Experience everything; learn from your experiences and the feedback that you get. Remember that there is no failure only feedback.

A few years ago, I fell in love with a man who looked like everything I had ever imagined I wanted. He was tall, dark and handsome with long, dark hair and a lean, muscular body. He had been in the SAS and was a karate champion. He was my own James Bond character, my Milk Tray man. How he made me laugh and helped me to believe in fairy tales again. All my usual cautions about how quickly to open my life and my heart to him evaporated in the excitement and passion of our meeting. I held nothing back and risked everything including my life, my children and my business. I let myself love and be loved, deeply. Nothing else mattered. My best friends and my family were afraid for me. They cautioned me to hold back, to take my time. I exposed myself to my colleagues, friends and family as a woman of deep, untidy feelings that could override my normal gift of being grounded and rational across all areas of my life.

The end of the relationship left me totally numb and hollow inside and I felt like the fool. And I would **do it all again**. I would not trade one moment of the passion for the protection of my pride. Why? Because through the experience I got some priceless learnings for myself. I learned what I really wanted in a relationship and I learned to be authentic, to be myself, because that is enough. That's what I mean when I say that I want you to experience everything. We do not die from being foolish. Why then do we fear it so much?

Life is not a rehearsal after all, so why then do so many people live it in that way, too afraid to take any risks and keeping their heads down in case someone spots their real potential? Enter into your life by stepping on to the stage, out of the Grey Zone, once and for all. Otherwise, as John Lennon memorably said, 'Life is what happens while you're busy making plans.'

One of my teachers, Peggy Dylan, describes our body as our prayer. It's how we relate to the world. If we see it as our prayer, why then do we abuse its well-being with alcohol and junk food, or keep it on a tight leash lest we have any amazingly innovative ideas that take us closer to our dreams? Think about it. How are you treating your body right now? How will **you** keep in balance whilst you pursue your goals? At the very least, take regular exercise, drink loads of water each day, eat a balanced diet and get enough sleep. That is the minimum requirement for someone pursuing their goals to keep their energy levels and well-being at their highest. See your life as a pathway to growth. If you do nothing there is no opportunity to learn. In contrast, if you accept the opportunities and challenges that come your way you will get the learnings that follow.

"Everyone needs to keep learning. Everyone needs goals.**"**

Richard Branson

Your proudest moments

As you start your journey now, focus each day on what you have achieved, rather than on those things that didn't go to plan. In one of my favourite songs, 'Proud', Heather Small asks: 'What have you done today to make you feel proud?' These do not have to be the biggest achievements of your life. They may be simple things like taking exercise, spending time with somebody you love, completing a task at work. For me, they are a mix of things that move me forward. I ask myself that question every day. Experiencing my life like that means that every day when I finally go to bed I reflect back and think that today was a good day. Are you ready to open your eyes and focus on your achievements?

Exercise 31

Keeping a diary of your proud moments

Keep a diary for a week of all your achievements during each day. Set yourself the challenge to ensure the list gets longer every day. As human beings, we more naturally focus on the things that don't go to plan. If you notice yourself doing that then, each day in your diary, set out two columns – one for the things you were proud of and the other for the things that you could do better next time. The only rule is that the list of things you are proud of must be longer.

As you record the things that you are proud of, notice how you begin to build new reference points for your belief system. Remember the analogy of building the house. Create new reference points and the old blocks fall away leaving the building very unstable. Perhaps you'll spot how much more successful you are than you thought or how good you really are at so many things. I know you'll notice things for the very first time that previously you were closed to.

Enlist support when you need it

On your journey towards your goals there will be times when the road seems rough and long. You may need some additional help at that moment to keep your momentum going. It saves you valuable time in the longer term.

If you need someone who is an 'expert' in the relevant field to work with you then this person is called a **mentor**. A mentor can provide you with technical support to keep you on track. A mentor will assist you in gathering the tools that you need to move closer to your goals. In organisations, high-potential staff are often provided with a mentor to guide them. I have worked with a mentor in the writing of this book. She is an expert in the field as she specialises in helping authors to write and publish books. She also has written books herself. At the start of my book we worked together to map out the key messages that I wanted to deliver. Since then, every week, we have reviewed my progress against the objectives and timescales I originally set for myself. I know that this has helped me to avoid lengthy and painful rewrites.

You may also get yourself a **coach**. The terms 'coach' and 'mentor' are often confused. A mentor is an expert and can be quite directive at times. In contrast, a coach is an expert facilitator, asking you questions until you come up with the answers for yourself. If you want someone to keep you on track and to assist you to break old patterns of procrastination and a lack of self-belief, then a coach may be better for you. I have also used a coach at times in my life when I needed to discover and break through limiting beliefs about myself and change old strategies. A coach can really assist you to become far more self-aware.

Lastly, find a model of excellence. I have already mentioned in this book how invaluable it is to find someone who has already achieved what you want to achieve and to find out how they did it. You do this by modelling their beliefs and strategies, and how they use their body (especially important when modelling sports people). In NLP terms, we would say that we model their:

- internal process, or how they do things
- internal state, or why they do things
- external behaviour, or what they do.

Give yourself time for self-reflection. My belief is that we absolutely benefit from understanding as much as we can about ourselves and the patterns and beliefs that we run. Working with others and taking time for self-reflection will allow you to grow and to develop. Remember: there is no failure only feedback. Next time you are in a situation that is significant, take your time to connect with the learnings. Ask a coach to assist you if possible. Take the time it takes before rushing off headstrong into the same challenges all over again. Give yourself the space for this and give it the priority it deserves.

Principles of success

We are almost at the end and there are just a few things more for me to say. First of all I'd like to summarise the key principles that we have discussed in this book and recommend that you memorise them and use them as your blueprint for success. When you follow this path you will succeed, and remember to keep going until you get your goals.

Principle 1 – get clear on your goal

Revisit the biggest goal you set at the start of this book. Double check that it really motivates you. Now check that your goal is specific, measurable, achievable, realistic and timed. Focus on your goal. Remember that whatever you put your attention on in your life will grow stronger.

Principle 2 – know why it is a must

What are your reasons for wanting to achieve this goal? Ask yourself, 'If I don't do this now what will it ultimately cost me?' Make sure that your goal is for you and that you're not achieving it for anyone else.

Principle 3 – take massive action

Are you prepared to do whatever it takes to achieve your goal, including things you do not want to do? Revisit your personal action plan. Take one small step and one large step today to begin to move towards your goal. Challenge yourself by asking if you are taking personal and 100 per cent responsibility for your goal. Are you at cause for your goal? Because, to the extent that you are not, you are giving your personal power away.

Principle 4 – know what you are getting

Be very aware of what works and what doesn't. Ask for feedback, and constantly evaluate your approach. Think of feedback as a gift and remember to learn from any action that doesn't go quite to plan.

Principle 5 – be prepared to change your approach

We've already come across saying that 'if you always do what you've always done, you'll always get what you've always got'! You must be prepared to be flexible, to move into the unknown. Security is an attachment to the known and the known is our past. No evolution in that. When you experience uncertainty you are on the right track – if you become too fixated on how to achieve your goal, you shut out a whole range of possibilities.

Principle 6 – ask for help from those who are already successful

When making major life changes, the most successful people in life model those who have already 'done it'. They do this by going on courses, being coached or simply asking for advice. You will probably find that with the appropriate support you will find the process of change more enjoyable, and your chances of success will be greatly increased.

There's not much more I can give to you. However, I've developed a light-hearted questionnaire that is designed to find out how far you have changed during the reading of this book and how determined you are to go for what you want. I suggest that you use the results as personal feedback about where you are right now as you begin your change journey and where you need to be. Have fun, enjoy and learn from the results.

My last word

Exercise 32

The 'Do you want it or what' quiz

1. Your friends describe you as:
   a. Determined
   b. Erratic
   c. Careful
   d. Focused on others.

---

2. You win £50,000 on the lottery. Do you:
   a. Invest it in your plans for the future?
   b. Spend it on your favourite car?
   c. Put it into a building society account?
   d. Give it to charity?

3. When you've got plans that are important to you, do you:
   a. Think about them all the time?
   b. Find your motivation level fluctuates?
   c. Focus on all the risks?
   d. Phone a friend for help?

4. You are given a year's free membership at your local gym as a gift. Do you:
   a. Get yourself into a routine and go regularly?
   b. Find it's impossible to get into a routine and so your visits drop off?
   c. Worry whether you should accept the gift?
   d. Give it away to a friend?

5. Your lover dumps you. Do you:
   a. Work out what you need to do differently next time?
   b. Blame them for everything?
   c. Pretend nothing's wrong?
   d. Give your friends the benefit of your experience?

6. How much do you believe you can really have what you want?
   a. Absolutely
   b. Some of the time
   c. Too anxious to totally commit
   d. Discuss with others before you answer.

7. You've just met the person of your dreams and fallen madly in love. The only trouble is, they live abroad. Do you:
   a. Find a way of being together?
   b. Not know whether to keep in touch?

    c. Think the whole idea is very risky?

    d. Dump them as you need to get home to feed your friend's goldfish?

8. When someone asks you for feedback, do you:

    a. Give it willingly?

    b. Make excuses to avoid the moment?

    c. Get very anxious even thinking about it?

    d. Worry that you may hurt their feelings?

9. At work you are asked to take on a tough new challenge. Do you:

    a. Say 'yes' immediately and feel excited about the prospect?

    b. Ask for two weeks to think about it?

    c. Turn it down because you don't know enough yet?

    d. Tell your boss to offer it to your best friend as she's more capable than you?

10. When you need help, do you:

    a. Actively seek out someone who can assist you?

    b. Ask everyone you know for advice?

    c. Worry about confidentiality?

    d. Find someone you can help out to make you feel better?

Add up the number of times you chose each letter, and then see below what the results say about you.

- **Highest score 'As' – congratulations – you really want it!** When you decide to move out of the Grey Zone, you are full of drive and enthusiasm. You focus your energies on what you want and you take responsibility for everything that happens to you. You have strong self-belief and confidence. You manage to stay motivated despite anything that happens and you've got optimism and the strength of will to see you through. You will succeed in whatever goals you set yourself. **Good luck** and remember always to **stay in the ring**.

- **Highest score 'Bs' – you can't make up your mind if you want it or not!** Sometimes you want to change and sometimes you don't. You do have great ideas that inspire you. The problem is that change takes consistency of effort and you'd really like to change if only it wasn't so difficult. You don't like to close down your options too early, which can lead to a scattergun approach as you go after your goals. You are not always on the 'C side', and if you can blame others when things go wrong you will. You must focus your energy on what you really want to allow you to succeed after finishing this book. Re-read Chapters 4 (Focus on what you want), 6 (Results or excuses?) and 7 (Believe you can).

- **Highest Score 'Cs' – it's too risky to want it!** You spend your days daydreaming about what it would be like to change. You have some dreams but they are for those people who are prepared to take risks. Well, if you always do what you've always done, you always get what you've always got. This is your moment of truth – **do you want it or what?** If the answer is really 'yes' then break your goal into small chunks and start to take action. Each small step will encourage you to go even further and before long you'll be surprised how much you've achieved. If the answer's 'no' then slip back into the Grey Zone where you can go unnoticed for the rest of your life. Re-read the whole book and this time take a deep breath and really go for it.

- **Highest score 'Ds' – you're too busy playing the best supporting role to want it!** Are you the person at the Oscars who would win best supporting actress or actor? Has it been easier to focus on someone else's problem than to work on your own? Well, look in the mirror and ask yourself whether it's time to step up to the task of taking responsibility for **what you want for yourself**. Some people, especially women, spend their entire lives focusing on what other people want – their husbands, their children, their elderly parents, etc. Do you want to look back and ask yourself the question 'What if?' If you're content with that it's up to you but I'm wondering why you've read this book. This is your moment of truth – **do you want it or what?** Take the first step. Say 'no' and notice how easy it is. After all, it's only a very small word. Take time for yourself. Start now by working out what you're going to do with the rest of your life. What's your legacy other than 'I was someone's partner, parent, friend, etc'? Do it now. It only takes one small step. And, if that's too much step down back into the Grey Zone and have a great life, but I doubt you will. Re-read the book and this time read it for yourself.

How did you get on with the questionnaire? Did you get some surprises? I have enjoyed being your tour guide but now it's time for you to embark on your own journey. I hope that I have inspired you to do something different with your life, to move outside of the Grey Zone towards the absolutely Brilliant Zone. That's where I'm heading and I want to meet you there. Remember that there is no 'try' – you either go for it or not – because anything less than 100 per cent effort is sabotage. Good luck, although I know that you won't need any as you have everything you need to be, do and have whatever you want. As Milton Erikson said, 'Let my voice go with you.' Enjoy the ride.

Come to the edge.
We might fall.
Come to the edge.
It's too high!
COME TO THE EDGE!
And they came
and he pushed
and they flew…

Christopher Logue

My moment of truth

As I stand at the foot of the glowing fire under the bright, full moon I ask myself if I'm really up to walking alone. It feels totally different without the energy of my friends to escort me across. I know that I can say that I walked but that would be letting myself down. This is one of those precious moments in life when you get the chance to prove to yourself that you are more than you thought you could be and I don't want to miss it! I feel my heart pounding and my whole body begins to tingle with excitement. The energy is rising throughout my body. Nothing in my life up until this moment seemed to be important any more. The fire ahead of me symbolises the rest of my life and how I choose to live it and what I want to achieve – so no pressure then...

I quietly focus on what I want to achieve. I want an amazing relationship, happy and healthy children, a successful business. I hear a voice in my head saying 'go for it!', yet my legs seem grounded right now and they just won't move. The heat from the fire is overwhelming and I'm afraid. I reassure myself by saying, 'You can do it', over and over again in my head. I'm standing literally at the foot of the fire and I hear nothing other than the beating of my heart and the wind through the trees. I begin to get frustrated with myself and I hear myself saying, 'You're ready.' This time it is a quiet energy that fills my body. I focus on a spot beyond the fire and visualise in my mind everything that I want to create in my life. I breathe in through my nose and out through my mouth three times and then I take that all-important first step into the unknown. I'm suddenly striding confidently over the fire. I can feel the heat under my feet and between my toes and I keep going. I take several more large steps and I'm over and on the other side. This time there is no one to whoop with just a quiet realisation that I've done it and I can do anything.

In those quiet few moments I proved to myself that I have the courage to face my fears and just do it! I feel very proud as I gently walk back up the hill. Number 12 is ready and waiting and I quietly whisper to them to cherish every moment.

What next?

The Change Corporation – our programmes

I hope that you have been inspired by this book. This is just the beginning! If you'd like to develop yourself further, and work personally with me, then here's what we do and how you can contact us.

Corporate programmes

Learning and development. Our clients include Unilever, DHL, Nokia, PriceWaterhouseCoopers, Durham Business School and Henley Management College. We offer bespoke programmes to meet your specific requirements in the areas of change management, leadership and team development.

Consultancy. We also provide change management consultants in our specialist areas of transformational change, culture change and organisation development.

Coaching

We offer life and executive coaching packages and we specialise in coaching senior female executives. We also offer a one-day Breakthrough session for those needing to resolve a particular issue FAST.

Open programmes

Change your life with NLP. Our three-hour taster workshop is run regularly. We show you how to use NLP to take control of your life and develop unstoppable self-confidence.

Three-day Powerful Presentations programme. Many people are more scared of speaking in public than almost anything else. This programme uses NLP to build your confidence and beliefs as a presenter. You learn how to present with charisma in any situation and get the results you want.

Ten-day Age with attitude. This is a unique programme for mid-life women who want more out of life and want to break away from any limiting beliefs that are holding them back right now. Far more than a personal development programme, AWA is about pursuing goals and achievements whether business or personal. The group comes together four times in 10 months so it's about long-term growth and not just a quick-fix. Delegates are also allocated their own personal coach to work with them in between modules. This programme is already being used by public-sector bodies, such as the NHS for the development of their female staff. Visit **www.agewithattitude.co.uk** for more information.

Seven-day Fast track NLP Practitioner, Practitioner of Time Line Therapy and Practitioner of Hypnotherapy. You will learn how to use NLP techniques to transform your own life and help others. Our practitioner programme allows you to become a Certified Practitioner of NLP in seven days, saving you 13 days of traditional classroom time. We do this by utilising pre-study CDs that you will then be able to use long after the training has finished as a helpful refresher. You will also study to become a Practitioner of Time Line Therapy™ and a Practitioner of Hypnosis.

Fourteen-day fast track NLP Master Practitioner, Master Practitioner of Time Line Therapy™ and Master Hypnotist. Our master practitioner programme will not only enable you to take your practitioner skills to a mastery level, it will also teach you many advanced techniques. Everything then comes together at the end of the programme through a breakthrough session where you will coach a client and be coached yourself through a truly transformational experience. You will also have the opportunity to become a Master Practitioner of Time Line Therapy™ and a Master Hypnotist. This programme also has a pre-study component.

More information is available at our websites:

www.thechangecorporation.com

www.lindseyagness.com

www.agewithattitude.co.uk

Email: info@thechangecorporation.com

Reading and films list

Reading

Agness, Lindsey, *Change Your Business with NLP*, Capstone Wiley, 2010

Agness, Lindsey, *Still 25 Inside*, Rodale MacMillan, 2010

Branson, Richard, *Screw it Let's Do it*, Virgin Books Ltd, 2006

Charvet, Shelle Rose, *Words that Change Minds*, Kendall Hunt Publishing Company, 1995, 1997

Chopra, Deepak, *Ageless Body, Timeless Mind*, Harmony Books, 1993

Covey, Stephen, *The 7 Habits of Highly Effective People*, Simon & Schuster, 1989

Csikszentmihalyi, Mihaly, *Flow*, Rider, 2002

Cumes, David, *Africa in My Bones*, South African Spearhead, 2004

Hay, Louisa, *You Can Heal Your Life*, Hay House Ltd, 1984

Hill, Napoleon, *Think and Grow Rich*, Random House Publishing Group, 1960

James, Tad and Woodsmall, Wyatt, *Timeline Therapy and the Basis of Personality*, Meta Publications, 1988

Knight, Sue, *NLP at Work*, Nicholas Brealey Publishing, 1995

Laborde, Genie Z. *Influencing with Integrity*, Crown House Publishing, 1998

Lewis, Byron and Pucelik, Frank, *Magic of NLP Demystified*, Metamorphous Press, 1993

Logue, Christopher, *Selected Poems of Logue*, Faber and Faber, 1996

Massey, Morris, *People Puzzle – Understanding Yourself*, Reston Publishing Company, 1979

Mehrabian, Albert, *Silent Messages*, Wadsworth Publishing Company, 1972

Meyer, Paul J., *Attitude is Everything (Attitude and Motivation Vol. 2)*, published by Paul J. Meyer, date unknown

Neill, Michael, *You Can Have What You Want*, Hay House Ltd, 2006

Pert, Candice, *Molecules of Emotion*, Simon & Schuster, 1998

Pierce, Penney, *The Intuitive Way: A Guide to Living from Inner Wisdom*, Axion Publishing, 1997

Robbins, Tony, *Unlimited Power, Unleash the Giant Within*, Simon & Schuster, 1991

The Three Initiates, *The Kybalion*, Cosmo Classics, 2006 (originally published 1912)

Tose, Paul and Mathison, Jane, *Neuro-Linguistic Programming: A Critical Appreciation for Managers and Developers*, Palgrave Macmillan, 2009

Films

What the Bleep Do We Know?, Captured Light and Lord of the Wind Films and Revolver Entertainment, 2004 (**www.thebleep.co.uk**)

The Secret, TS Production LLC, 2006 (**www.the secret.tv**)

Appendix 1: My meta programmes

Answers:

Q1 (a) Proactive (b) Reactive

Q2 (a) Internal (b) External

Q3 (a) Sameness (b) Difference

Q4 (a) Specific (b) Global

Q5 (a) Attention on others (b) Attention on self

Q6 (a) Options (b) Procedures

Q7 (a) Inferential (b) Literal (listener)

Q8 (a) Literal (b) Inferential (speaker)

Proactive/Reactive

Proactive people

Proactive people like to get on with things. They are more likely to take responsibility for making things happen and they will certainly take over if others around them are seen to be too 'slow'. They enjoy action and getting stuff done.

Words and phrases they might use: Let's do it; it's time; focus; action

Reactive people

They prefer to wait for others to make the first move, and like to explore all the consequences of taking action before taking any. Often this means life has moved on and left them behind. They won't make a move unless they are 100 per cent convinced that it's the right thing to do.

Words and phrases they might use: There's no rush, let's see what others do first, what will happen if I do/don't take action, think about it, wait

Internal/External

Internal people

Internal people evaluate things on the basis of what *they* think is appropriate. They provide their own motivation and make their own decisions. They decide what they want to do and how they will go about doing it. They can be quite opinionated and have difficulty accepting other people's direction and feedback. These people like to decide for themselves. They have difficulty accepting either feedback or praise. They respond best to phrases like, 'Only you can decide to ...'.

Words and phrases they might use: Let's do it this way; that's the way it's done; I just know.

External people

External people need external feedback to feel good about themselves. Other sources provide the information which they accept. They need external standards and feedback. These people need to be managed. They need to know what to do and how to do it. They need feedback and praise (or constructive criticism).

Words and phrases they might use: Tell me what you think; let me know; give me some feedback; was it OK?.

Sameness/Difference

Sameness people

Sameness people will first notice the similarities and then notice differences. They may discuss how things have gradually changed over time. They like things to remain relatively the same. They are not comfortable with change unless it occurs slowly and gradually. They talk about how things are the same. They will discuss same or common features or things that have not changed. They will respond better to things that are 'improved, better, or slightly more advanced', but they will resist things that are new.

Words and phrases they might use: 'same; same as; in common; keep the same; maintain; better; same except; evolved; gradual; evolutionary

Difference people

Difference people will notice things that are different from or mismatch what they have noticed previously. They like change and variety. They don't like static or stable situations. Change doesn't have to be revolutionary, but it does have to happen. Often they are constantly reorganising. Most will notice the differences first, and then the similarities.

Words and phrases they might use: new; different; changed; unusual

Specific/Global

Specific people

Specific people give you all of the small details and will go down several levels in explaining. They are comfortable with and able to understand small pieces of data. They talk with and about sequences. They prefer things to be arranged in sequences. When they describe something they will talk about the steps in the event. If interrupted, they will often go back to the first step. They are not able to make sense of the larger picture and often have difficulty with priorities.

With these people it's best to break things down into specifics and stress the details.

Words and phrases they might use: exactly; specifically; precisely; first – second – then – next

Global people

Global people give you the big picture without any of the details. They will describe a situation in random order without using proper nouns or extra modifiers. They are most comfortable with large chunks of information. They make sense of the world in terms of the overall framework of a situation, usually seeing the whole project at once. They can conceive of and work with the parts as necessary, but they usually see them as random bits of the larger framework. They tend to speak in simple sentences with few prepositional phrases. If you present too many details, they will ask you what it means or ask you to move on. However, you should expect that they may fill in the details differently from the way you would.

Words and phrases they might use: generally; overview; big picture; framework

Attention on others/Self

Attention on others people

You can always tell a person with attention on others because they are interested in what's going on around them and they like to find out about people. They have their attention 'outside' of themselves and are good at building rapport with others. They tend to be quite animated individuals and they take notice of what others are doing. They are the kind of people you'd want as cabin crew on an airline.

Words and phrases they might use: Can I help? How are you? What do you need? I noticed you were looking x'd

Attention on self people

In contrast, attention on self people are very inward facing. You could drop something in front of them and they would be unlikely to look up. They are that person behind the counter at the local shop who seems to 'ignore' you for ages whilst they get on with what they are doing first without even noticing you are there. These people tend to miss non-verbal clues and make short responses to you when they do notice you there.

Words and phrases they might use: Sorry didn't see you there; What was it that you wanted? I'm busy at the moment, can it wait?

Options/Procedures

Options people

These people tend to be focused on a goal. They are glass 'half-full' characters. They like to have possibilities and options available to them. They enjoy feeling they have a choice about what they do. They are good motivators of other people as their enthusiasm is infective.

Words and phrases they might use: focus; goals; let's go for it; there are many possibilities; opportunities for the future; choices

Procedures people

These people don't feel that they have a lot of choice about how they lead their lives. They often have the weight of the world on their shoulders. They are more likely to be glass 'half-empty' people. They believe they have to do what they do – maybe because of family responsibilities or pressure to follow the family business. They may see the risks in things as they like to follow procedures and rules.

Words and phrases they might use: Here are the procedures we need to follow to get the best result; Let's do this in an orderly fashion; I have to do things this way

Inferential/Literal (listening style)

Inferential listeners

They infer things from what is said. They are great mind readers and often jump to the wrong conclusions. They also think that any question is a request for action.

Words and phrases they might use: I thought you wanted me to do something; I thought that's what you meant

Literal listeners

They take what is said very literally. If you want something done, you would need to ask them very directly or they are likely to ignore you. For example, literal listeners may not know when an inferential speaker compliments them.

Words and phrases they might use: If you want me to do something please tell me; What specifically do you want me to do?

Literal/Inferential (speaking style)

Literal speakers

Literal speakers will be very direct, almost to the point of being rude. They will find giving feedback easy. They like to come to the point very quickly and not mess about with hints and tips. You will always know where you stand with these people though you may not like it.

Words and phrases they might use: this is what you did well; this is what you need to improve on; you are not performing as you should because...

Inferential speakers

These people feel awkward about being too direct. They worry about upsetting people. Often they waste a lot of time giving 'hints and tips' or implying that something is wrong. A literal speaker would get very frustrated when communicating with an inferential speaker.

Words and phrases they might use: I don't like the way they behave, do you? What do you think about the latest fashions this year? Have you tried that new deodorant?

Appendix 2: The language used by different representational systems

Visual	Kinaesthetic	Auditory	Audio digital
see	feel	hear	sense
look	touch	listen	experience
appear	grasp	sound(s)	understand
view	get hold of	make music	think
show	slip through	harmonise	learn
dawn	catch on	tune in/out	process
reveal	tap into	be all ears	decide
envision	make contact	rings a bell	motivate
illuminate	throw out	silence	consider
twinkle	turn around	be heard	change
clear	hard	resonate	perceive
foggy	unfeeling	deaf	insensitive
focused	concrete	mellifluous	distinct
hazy	scrape	dissonance	conceive
crystal clear	get a handle on	overtones	know
flash	solid	unhearing	question
imagine	suffer	attune	be conscious
picture	unbudging	outspoken	logic
sparkling	impression	tell	reasonable
snap shot	touch base	announce	statistically
vivid	rub	talk	
perceive	smooth	speak	
light	pushy	resonate	
ray	stumble	state	
mesmerise	in touch	whine	
watch	relaxed	babble	

perspective	loose	echo
frame	cool	orchestrate
shine	tepid	whisper
dim	heavy	snap
image		hum
vision		loud
observe		dialogue

Used with permission. © The Tad James Co, Tad and Adriana James.

The Bestselling Book on NLP

David Molden & Pat Hutchinson

brilliant

NLP

What the most successful people know, do and say

9780273732556

2nd Edition

Brilliant NLP clearly explains how NLP works, giving you plenty of exercises to help you put theory into practice so you'll be more than equipped to take control, change your thinking and change your life.

Brilliant Outcomes:

✓ Understand and master NLP step by step

✓ Discover how to apply NLP to your life, right now

✓ Change your thinking; change your life

Available from **www.pearson-books.com** and all good bookshops